# Monetary and Fiscal Policy and Business Cycles in the Modern Era

D1503035

Alan L. Sorkin
University of Maryland

**Lexington Books**
*D.C. Heath and Company/Lexington, Massachusetts/Toronto*

**Library of Congress Cataloging-in-Publication Data**

Sorkin, Alan L.
  Monetary and fiscal policy and business cycles in
the modern era.

  Includes index.
  1. Business cycles.   2. Monetary policy.   3. Fiscal
policy.   I. Title.
HB3711.S6234   1988        338.5'42        88-12872
ISBN 0-669-13386-8 (alk. paper)
ISBN 0-669-19644-4 (pbk. : alk. paper)

Published simultaneously in Canada
Printed in the United States of America
Casebound International Standard Book Number: 0-669-13386-8
Paperbound International Standard Book Number: 0-669-19644-4
Library of Congress Catalog Card Number: 88-12872

The paper used in this publication meets the minimum requirements of American National
Standard for Information Sciences—Permanence of Paper for Printed Library Materials,
ANSI Z39.48-1984. ∞™

    89  90  91  92  8  7  6  5  4  3  2

# Contents

# Tables

# Figures

## DC Heath
A Raytheon Company

## LEXINGTON BOOKS - REVIEW COPY

| QUAN. | CATALOG NUMBER | TITLE | PUB. DATE | LOCATION | PRICE |
|---|---|---|---|---|---|
| 1 | 015828-3 | AMERICAN MONETARY SYSTEM PB | | 2BB0402 | 16.95 |
| 1 | 019644-4 | MONETARY & FISCAL POL & BUS CY PB | | 2AA4802 | 14.95 |

**NO CHARGE - REVIEW COPY**

IF THIS BOOK WAS SENT FOR YOUR REVIEW, PLEASE SEND 2 COPIES OF YOUR
REVIEW TO: LEXINGTON BOOKS - REVIEW EDITOR
D.C. HEATH AND COMPANY
125 SPRING STREET
LEXINGTON, MASSACHUSETTS 02173

# Preface and Acknowledgments

The business cycle is an important and deeply embedded feature of industrial economies in which free enterprise is the dominant form of business organization. Cyclical fluctuations in economic activity have a major impact on jobs and income with concomitant effects on the standard of living of the typical individual. Business cycles have political implications as well. Incumbent politicians are more likely to be reelected during periods of prosperity as compared to those of economic decline. Thus, President Reagan's landslide victory over Walter Mondale can be partially attributed to the rapid economic recovery in 1983 and 1984 from the effects of the 1981–1982 recession.

In recent years there have been several highly technical, econometrically oriented books published in the fields of business cycles and monetary and fiscal policy. While these studies have provided important contributions to knowledge, they were often incomprehensible to nonspecialists or even to specialists who were untrained in mathematical economics or econometrics.

This nontechnical book can be used for a variety of purposes. For example, it can be assigned as a supplemental text in a macroeconomic theory course in which the instructor wishes to place some emphasis on business cycles and related policy issues. It may prove beneficial to students in money and banking and public policy courses who wish to combine a knowledge of cycles with information on monetary and fiscal policy. Finally, members of the college-educated general public with an interest in economic fluctuations may perhaps find this book worthwhile reading.

Iris Batchellor and Peggy Bremer typed the several drafts of the manuscript in a most excellent manner. The manuscript was copyedited by Sara Held, and David and Linda Buskus prepared the index.

# 1
# Introduction

During the late 1960s and early 1970s many academic, governmental, and private economists expressed "the conviction that business cycles were not inevitable, that government policy could and should keep the economy close to a path of steady real growth at a constant target rate of unemployment."[1]

Of course, some minor fluctuations in economic activity were not considered an impossible occurrence. Economists generally agreed, however, that these variations in business activity were more the result of political mistakes and occasional errors in economic forecasting than of inadequate knowledge of how the economy functioned. In short, economists believed that the business cycle had been eliminated. Although the handling of the economic consequences of the Vietnam War raised questions about the efficacy of the tools of economic stabilization, these doubts were connected more to the political controversy associated with that conflict than to actual economic misjudgments. By the early 1970s, the persistence of strong inflationary pressures, even in the face of mild recession, began to raise serious concerns; the responses of the economy to changes in monetary and fiscal policy no longer seemed very predictable. Yet it was not until the 1973–1975 recession, the most severe in the post–World War II period, that the lessons of the so-called "New Economics" of the 1960s were seriously challenged.

Now, more than a decade after the end of that severe worldwide recession, many countries in the industrialized world are still faced with a combination of high levels of unemployment and persistent inflation. There is uncertainty and disagreement about how the economy responds to changes in budget deficits and the money supply. The earlier confidence in our ability to maintain the economy on a smooth upward path close to full employment is gone.

There are nevertheless substantial reasons to believe the economy can avoid declines similar in magnitude to the Great Depression of the 1930s. However, the evidence strongly suggests that there is some tendency toward fluctuations in business activity over relatively long periods of time—for example, periods of ten to twenty years.

Such swings in economic activity may be influenced by a number of more or less objective events, such as changes in population, wars and their repercussions, and waves of technological innovation. Variations in business activity also appear to be influenced by less tangible, even psychological, phenomena. For example, a long period of prosperity breeds confidence, and confidence results in new standards of what is prudent and what is risky.

For a time the process is self-reinforcing: it sustains investment and risk taking. Eventually the situation becomes self-correcting, as natural limits to some of the factors supporting the economic advance are reached, and further gains cannot occur readily. The nation finds itself with more houses and retail stores and interstate trucks and steel capacity than we can fully utilize. Financial positions are extended, and the economy becomes more vulnerable to adverse and unexpected occurrences. In this situation, it becomes apparent that a business decline cannot be dealt with as readily by policy changes that were relatively successful in a period of economic expansion. The economic mood grows conservative and uncertain: we rediscover the business cycle.[2]

Viewed from this perspective, one need only consider human nature to find some explanation for recurrent swings in business activity in a market economy. There is a natural tendency to assume that what one has observed for a period of years can be readily projected into the future. However, as we act on these assumptions and expectations—and as the memories of earlier experience fade, our approach changes. When this occurs, new forces and new conditions arise that invalidate the assumptions upon which we are operating.

## The Forces for Stability

The Great Depression of the 1930s resulted in considerable economic, financial, and social legislation designed both to restore prosperity and to insulate the economy from future depression. The success in terms of the first objective remains debatable, for it was not until after World War II began that the nation's unemployment rate fell below 10 percent. However, many of the measures introduced in that earlier period, which were extended and strengthened after World War II, still provide considerable protection against a major downturn in business activity.

The creation of the Federal Deposit Insurance Corporation (FDIC) in 1933 is a good example. By insuring most depositors against loss, the FDIC has prevented or sharply reduced mass withdrawals from banks by individuals fearing that they would be unable to withdraw their deposits if the bank became insolvent. Historically, isolated weaknesses in the banking system, perhaps caused by defaults on loans in a business downturn, could put heavy pressure on even relatively sound institutions. This resulted in the elimination of sources of credit and seriously worsened economic conditions. In fact rising numbers of bank failures had been a major feature of earlier serious business contractions, including the 1907–1908 recession and the severe 1929–1933 decline, which was a major part of the Great Depression.

Until recently, the postwar period has been relatively free of bank failures. However, in 1985–1987, the FDIC had to compensate depositors following the failure of a few large banks and a somewhat larger number of small institutions.[3] The depositors, virtually without exception, received the full value of their deposits from the FDIC. The losses were limited almost entirely to stockholders of the affected banks.

Another reform in the financial area was the creation of the Securities and Exchange Commission. An appropriate motto for this agency might be "Truth in Borrowing."[4] While the results are more difficult to discern than in the case of the FDIC, some of the worst speculative excesses in financial markets (such as those seen in the late 1920s), as well as the outright fraud that characterized some earlier periods, have been greatly reduced.

Perhaps even more important in terms of assisting economic stability have been the new social programs originating in the 1930s that help protect the individual from the financial consequences of loss of employment or provide support during retirement. For example, a combined state and federal unemployment insurance program provides financial assistance for six to twelve months at a substantial fraction of normal pay for those laid off from jobs. Social Security (now taxable) provides the elderly with funds for support whether or not they have personal savings available. These programs reduce the sensitivity of consumer spending to *current* income and production, thereby presumably moderating the cumulating forces that can deepen and extend a business decline.

The above are, in a sense, passive policies; their moderating effects are triggered more or less automatically by fluctuations in business activity. The Employment Act of 1946, committing the federal government to take positive discretionary actions to counteract unemployment, embodied a more activist approach. The following is the essence of the act's declaration of policy: "The Congress hereby declares that it is the continuing responsibility of the federal government to use all practicable means . . . to promote maximum employment, production and purchasing power."[5] Its intellectual origins lay in the Keynesian revolution (see Chapter 3) and in the view that the federal government had failed to utilize fiscal policy to deal adequately with the problems of the Great Depression. It could also be interpreted symbolically as the end of the principle of yearly balanced budgets.

Along with these new legislative and policy approaches, the middle part of the twentieth century saw some important changes in economic structure and the composition of national income that economists generally believed would contribute to stability. One important change was the increasing role of government in total spending. In 1929 federal spending on goods and services amounted to only 1.4 percent of gross national product (GNP). By 1950 the federal government's share was up to 6.5 percent of GNP, and by 1986 to 8.8 percent. Counting all expenditures—transfers of various types as well as purchases—the percentage rose from 2.5 percent in 1929 to 23.8 percent by 1986.[6]

Government spending is relatively insensitive to changes in business activity; in fact the so-called automatic stabilizers, such as unemployment insurance, work countercyclically. Thus, the increased role of government and decreased relative size of the private sector are moderating factors in regard to cyclical economic fluctuations. To a degree, the increases in state and local spending after World War II acted similarly, although that type of spending is not so insensitive to economic conditions as that of the federal government.

Another stabilizing mechanism can be found in the revenue side of the federal budget. Reliance on corporate and individual income tax as a source of revenue has sharply increased. In 1929 income tax revenues were only 2.3 percent of GNP whereas by 1986 they had risen to 9.8 percent.[7]The significance is that income taxes fluctuate with changes in income. Thus, for example, when income decreases, income tax liabilities decline more than proportionally (due to the progressive nature of the tax system). Consequently, both the consumer and private firms find income losses cushioned to some degree in recession; the cushioning helps to maintain consumer purchases and to a lesser extent investment spending.

One factor within the private sector operates in the same stabilizing direction. Fewer workers today are directly employed in goods-producing activities than in the past. Moreover, the growth in planning, in research and development, and in computer-assisted record-keeping have made the white collar segment a larger fraction of the work force. Many white collar workers are necessary regardless of the level of output, making them in effect a "quasi-fixed" factor of production. This changing composition of the work force serves to diminish the speed and magnitude of layoffs relative to declines in output. The consequences for corporate profits in periods of recession are adverse, but the overall rate of consumer spending is likely to be sustained.

In 1966 Peter Elibott estimated the particular impact of automatic stabilizers such as the income tax and the unemployment insurance program. He found that over the 1948–1960 period, downturns were between 30 and 50 percent less severe than if the stabilizers had been absent.[8] Using a more global approach, E. Philip Howrey measured the overall multiplier effect of exogenous spending and its impact on GNP. He found some evidence that the multiplier had dropped significantly after World War II.[9] The role of government is largely responsible for the decline in dynamic multipliers implied by large scale econometric models from multipliers of four or five in prewar data to two or less in postwar data.[10]

## The "Death" of the Business Cycle

Following World War II, fear of a serious business decline was widespread. The severe downturn of 1920–1921 that followed World War I suggested to many that the post–World War II period would bring similar conditions. In fact, the major problem immediately after the war turned out not to be recession; it was inflation. The latter was due to the postwar shortage of goods and a high level of consumer spending. Despite the low interest rates, however, common stocks were valued at well under ten times earnings, suggesting pessimism in regard to future profits.

While a recession did occur in 1948–1949, it proved to be much milder than expected. Real GNP fell by only about 1.5 percent and the unemployment rate rose to only 7.9 percent, far less than the levels reached in the 1930s or even in the post–World War I downturn. In addition, the recession was of fairly brief duration.

The postwar rearmament and the Korean conflict soon produced much larger government spending, and concerns about the underlying stability of the economy persisted. Another recession occurred after the Korean War ended, the downturn of 1953–1954. This recession was also relatively mild. Fears about the inevitability of a major depression receded, and changing expectations were reflected in part by a sustained upsurge in stock prices and price/earnings ratios.

By 1961, there had been four postwar recessions. In fact, recessions occurred as frequently after World War II as they did before the war. However, none of the postwar recessions had been severe. Government policy makers believed that the automatic stabilizers and discretionary monetary and fiscal policy as well as institutional safeguards had greatly reduced the likelihood of a severe business downturn.

Then came the long period of business expansion of 1961–1969. The expansion lasted more than one hundred months and exceeded all previous records for longevity. Government economists attributed this sustained period of prosperity to the correct mix of policy instruments. The innovative tax credit of 1962 was followed by an investment boom. More importantly, the large tax cuts (by 1964 standards) seemed timed to sustain a business upswing during a period when many past recoveries had come to an end.

Simultaneously, less dramatic changes in spending programs were aimed at long-term problems such as structural unemployment and the balance of payments deficit. As the economy continued to grow, so did the public's confidence in the ability of economists to fine-tune the economy and keep it on an upward trend.

There was one economic difficulty during this period. Rising defense spending at the time of the Vietnam buildup had not been anticipated. Offsetting monetary and fiscal policies were not undertaken quickly enough and rising prices eventually accompanied increased prosperity. Economists did not accept the blame for the Vietnam War–induced inflation. They claimed that they had been misled about the size of defense expenditures and that their advice (primarily to raise taxes) was rejected due to its political unacceptability. Subsequent inflationary pressure proved that if President Johnson had accepted their advice, inflation in the late 1960s and early 1970s would have been reduced. Monetary and fiscal policies did finally tighten, but this policy change was too long in coming.

Moreover, when the economy appeared to weaken in late 1966, fiscal and monetary policy became stimulative, and the slowdown in the upward trend of economic activity did not become a recession because the economy never experienced an absolute decline.

It is difficult at present to recapture the sense of optimism and confidence that characterized that time. As Arthur Okun said, "When recessions were a regular feature of the economic environment, they were often viewed as inevitable. . . . Recessions are now considered fundamentally preventable like airplane crashes and unlike hurricanes."[11]

Walter Heller, chairman of the Council of Economic Advisors in the first half of the 1960s, argued in 1969 that there was

> a constantly deepening conviction in the business and financial community that alert and active fiscal-monetary policy will keep the economy operating at a higher proportion of its potential in the future than in the past; that beyond short and temporary slowdowns, or perhaps even a recession—that's not ruled out in this vast and dynamic economy of ours—lies the prospect of sustained growth in that narrow band around full employment.[12]

It seemed entirely appropriate that the Department of Commerce chose to cease calling its monthly statistical publication *Business Cycle Developments* in favor of *Business Conditions Digest*. The content was the same, but the expectations had changed. Moreover, it was not just the attitude of economists and bureaucrats that had changed, but also that of businessmen and consumers.

## The Disillusionment

A mild recession did occur in 1969–1970, the fifth of the postwar period. The business decline did little to weaken the basic faith that the U.S. economy had become invulnerable to major downturns, for it was again mild and of relatively short duration. Then in 1973, inflation became severe. The accelerated rate of price increase seemed to be caused primarily by several unrelated events—a shortage of grain, the oil crisis, and devaluation of the dollar. The problems they posed seemed difficult but not unmanageable in terms of sustaining growth and employment.

The optimism was finally eliminated by the severe recession that began in November 1973 and became a rapid decline by late in 1974. It turned out to be the most severe economic contraction of the post–World War II period. Real GNP declined by 6 percent, about twice as much as the next largest postwar recession, the 1953–1954 downturn, and almost four times as great as the average decline of real GNP during the five previous postwar recessions. From the end of 1973 until May 1975, the unemployment rate rose by more than 4 percentage points, reaching 9 percent. This was far above the level previously experienced during the postwar period. It represented a degree of joblessness that would have been considered not only highly unlikely but intolerable a few years earlier.[13]

Moreover, the experience overseas was, in general, similar to that in this country. In nearly every industrialized country, many of which had been virtually free of recession in the earlier postwar period, unemployment reached postwar highs.

The very severity of the recession also helped expose some financial weaknesses that were not characteristic of earlier post–World War II recessions. These weaknesses were reflected most clearly in unusually large loan losses experienced by banks.

By the standards of severe contractions in the past (1920–1921, 1929–1933, and 1937–1938), the 1973–1975 recession can be considered relatively mild. For example, from 1929 to 1933 real GNP fell by 30 percent. Even during the 1937–1938 downturn, total output declined 9 percent. The unemployment rate in those three pre–World War II depressions increased considerably. It rose about 8 percentage points during the 1920–1921 and 1937–1938 downturns (about twice the increase of 1973–1975) and by 24 percentage points during the 1929–1933 contraction. Moreover, in a qualitative sense, despite some strains and problems, the financial structure held firm in 1973–1975—a sharp contrast to earlier experience during major contractions. Thus, one can maintain that our existing policies and institutions have insulated the economy from severe cumulating downturns[14] even if they are unable to prevent the occurrence of recession.

Since the severe 1973–1975 recession the economy has never returned to full employment. In the late 1970s unemployment was nearly as high as the peak levels of earlier recessions. The recessions of 1980 and 1981–1982 pushed unemployment to 12 million in November 1982, or 10.8 percent of the labor force. Even with more than five years of fairly strong economic growth, unemployment in February 1988 was more than 7 million, or 5.7 percent of the labor force.

The 1975–1983 period was characterized by high inflation and high unemployment. The combination of these phenomena, known as "stagflation," reflected a situation where economic growth was slow or (from 1979 to 1982) nonexistent. Productively gains in industry were far below historical averages and higher wages led to increased labor costs and higher prices.

Macroeconomists found that traditional monetary and fiscal policies seemed to have little impact in a period of stagflation. The relatively broad consensus that existed in the 1960s regarding the role of various macroeconomic policies has been undermined by the economic events of the past fifteen years. Policy recommendations today seem to reflect political idelogy as much as they reflect economic theory.

The 1983–1988 upswing in the business cycle was sixty-one months old as of January 1988, with forecasts indicating continuing economic growth throughout 1988. However, unlike the mid-1960s, there is no longer serious discussion regarding the elimination of the business cycle even though the current expansion is the longest in peacetime history.

Thus, the economic events of the past ten years have been sobering. Economists no longer think they have all the answers in regard to questions of economic policy or business fluctuations. This has resulted in a more cautious set of business practices, which if nothing else may result in a relatively mild economic downturn when one occurs.

An example of this trend is capital investment, which remained relatively restrained until the 1983–1988 business expansion was well under way. The relationships between capital utilization and investment typical of the mild postwar recessions would point to substantially higher spending on plant and equipment than has in fact developed. Inventory behavior has also been cautious. Businesses have reacted very quickly to rising stock/sales ratios, with the result that a kind of mini-adjustment has slowed the advance during parts of nearly every year of the current recovery.

In general, financial management has also returned to a more conservative pattern. Corporations replaced much short-term debt with debt of a longer maturity and built up liquid assets as well. While the changes are not dramatic, banks appear to have reappraised some lending policies (particularly with regard to developing countries), and growth has become less of a management imperative. A number of states and localities, sometimes under severe financial pressure, have been working toward a more conservative set of financial practices.

## Plan of This Book

The second chapter considers the major characteristics of the business cycle. Cycle length, leading, coincident, and lagging indicators of business fluctuations, and the economic activity associated with the various phases of the cycle are discussed.

Chapter three presents some of the major business cycle theories that have been developed in the past one hundred years. These include classical theories, the cycle theory of Keynes, and selected post-Keynesian contributions. The principal strengths and weaknesses of each theory are assessed.

The next chapter considers each of the eight postwar business cycles. The role that monetary and fiscal policies played in their amelioration as well as some of the causes of each cycle are critically discussed.

Chapter 5 deals with some important effects of business cycles. Business cycles have important effects on total output and employment. Certain categories of workers are more vulnerable to recession than others. The final portion of the chapter examines the negative impact of business cycle downturns on health status.

The sixth chapter explores the use of monetary policy as a stabilization tool. The various types of monetary policies are discussed within the context of the Federal Reserve System. The chapter concludes with a review of recent monetary policy.

The final chapter is concerned with the other major tool of stabilization policy, namely fiscal policy. Both automatic stabilizers and discretionary activities such as public works programs are examined. The problem of massive government deficits is also considered, together with the relationship between the budget deficit and the trade deficit.

## Notes

1. James Tobin, *The New Economics One Decade Older* (Princeton, N.J.: Princeton University Press, 1974), p. 7.

2. Paul Volcker, *The Rediscovery of the Business Cycle*, The Charles C. Moskowitz Memorial Lectures (New York: Free Press, 1978), p. 29.

3. Franklin Edwards, "Can Regulatory Reform Prevent the Impending Disaster in Financial Markets?" in *Restructuring the Financial System: A Symposium Sponsored by the Federal Reserve Bank of Kansas City* (Kansas City, Mo.: Federal Reserve Bank of Kansas City, 1987), p. 16.

4. Volcker, op.cit., p. 31.

5. U.S. Congress, Joint Economic Committee, *Employment Act of 1946, as Amended, with Related Laws*, 89th Cong. 2d sess. (Washington, D.C.: U.S. Government Printing Office, 1966), p. 1.

6. U.S. Department of Commerce, *Economic Report of the President*, 1987 (Washington, D.C.: U.S. Government Printing Office, 1987), pp. 256 and 331.

7. Ibid., pp. 252 and 333.

8. Peter Elibott, "The Effectiveness of Automatic Stabilizers," *American Economic Review* 56, no. 3 (June 1966): pp 450–65.

9. E. Philip Howrey, "Structural Change and Postwar Economic Stability: An Econometric Test," *Review of Economics and Statistics* 52, no. 1 (February 1970): 18–25.

10. Bert Hickman and Robert Coen, *An Annual Growth Model of the United States Economy* (Amsterdam: North Holland Press, 1976), p. 194.

11. Arthur Okun, *The Political Economy of Prosperity* (Washington, D.C.: The Brookings Institution, 1970), p. 33.

12. Milton Friedman and Walter Heller, *Monetary vs. Fiscal Policy: A Dialogue* (New York: Graduate School of Business of New York University, 1969), p. 31.

13. Volcker, p. 40.

14. Ibid., p. 41.

# 2
# Characteristics of the Business Cycle

This chapter discusses the major concepts associated with the business cycle. These include the phases of the cycle and alternative views of the length of the typical cycle as well as the principal features of cyclical behavior. Some international aspects of the business cycle are also discussed.

Two of the leading American contributors to business cycle analysis are Wesley Mitchell and Arthur Burns. The former played a major role in the founding of the National Bureau of Economic Research in 1920, while the latter recently retired from a long career of academic and public service that included the chairmanship of the Federal Reserve Board.

As Burns and Mitchell indicated:

> Business cycles are a type of fluctuation found in the aggregate economic activity of nations that organize their work mainly in business enterprises. A cycle consists of expansions occurring at about the same time in many economic activities, followed by similarly general recessions, contractions, and revivals which merge into the expansion phase of the next cycle; this sequence of changes is recurrent but not periodic; in duration business cycles vary from more than one year to ten or twelve years. They are not divisible into shorter cycles of similar character with amplitudes approximately their own.[1]

The term *business cycle* is slightly misleading because movements in output and related economic indicators do not occur at perfectly regular intervals. These aggregates, however, move with a degree of regularity that has been observed for many years. Business fluctuations vary greatly in scope as well as duration, yet they have certain features in common. First, they are national or international in scope. Second, they affect output, employment, retail sales, residential and nonresidential construction, and other macroeconomic variables. Third, they are persistent, meaning that they last for several years. In general, the upward movement in business

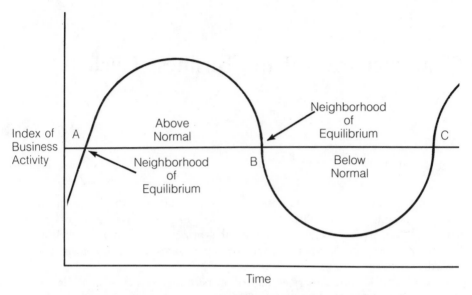

**Figure 2–1. Schumpeter's Neighborhoods of Equilibrium**

activity lasts for a longer period of time than the downturn. This fact is well established by the historical chronologies of business cycles that have occurred in the United States, Great Britain, France, and Germany.

## Phases of the Cycle

Burns and Mitchell regarded the *peaks* and *troughs* as the critical mark-off points in the cycle.[2] Accordingly the phases of the cycle can be divided into two components: the *expansion* phase extending from trough to peak and the *contraction* phase extending from peak to trough. There are, in addition, the lower and upper turning points, of relatively short duration. At the lower turning point, *revival* begins and grows rapidly into the expansion phase. At the upper turning point *recession* overtakes the economy and soon develops into the contraction phase. Thus, the cycle is regarded as consisting of four closely interrelated phases: (1) revival, (2) expansion, (3) recession, and (4) contraction.

Schumpeter believed that the critical points are to be found, not in the peaks and troughs of the cycle, but at or near the "points of inflection" (see fig. 2–1).[3] A, B, and C are points of inflection around which cluster the areas or "neighborhoods of equilibrium." The farther the economy moves

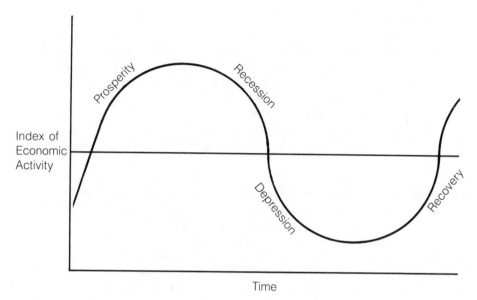

**Figure 2–2. Schumpeter's Four-Phase Cycle**

(up or down) from the neighborhood of equilibrium, the stronger become the forces that prevent further cumulative upward (or downward) movement and pull the economy back to equilibrium. In the portion of the cycle extending from A to B, economic activity is relatively high; this period may be regarded as the "good" years. The period extending from B to C, when economic activity is running below average, may be considered the "poor" years.

Schumpeter's analysis involves a *four-phase cycle* of (1) prosperity, (2) recession, (3) depression, (4) recovery (fig. 2–2). The upper half of the phase cycle is divided into two parts: *prosperity* and *recession*. In the prosperity phase, employment will continue to increase, but at a decreasing rate, until the peak of the cycle is reached. In the recession phase, employment will decrease at an accelerating rate until the point of inflection is reached. From this point on, the cycle moves into the lower half of the four-phase cycle, which may be divided into two phases: *depression* and *recovery*. During the depression phase, employment will continue declining, but at a gradually decreasing rate, until the trough of the cycle is reached. During the recovery phase, employment will grow at an increasing rate up to the point of inflection.[4]

For Burns and Mitchell, the turning points were to be regarded as more meaningful than Schumpeter's cumulative processes that oscillate around the "neighborhoods of equilibrium."

## The Juglar, Kitchin and Kondratieff Cycles

Clement Juglar, who published his findings in the 1860s, was one of the first economists to collect and analyze statistical data and to conclude that what others had viewed as isolated panics and depressions were really only phases of a continuous cycle. He was the first to write about the business cycle in terms of three phases: prosperity, crisis, and liquidation.[5] He reported the typical cycle as having an average duration of nine to ten years, though he was careful to avoid any assertion that the cycle was periodic in nature.

In 1923 Joseph Kitchin developed the thesis that business cycles are really of two types—major and minor.[6] The minor cycle, he suggested, has an average duration of approximately 40 months. This he termed the primary cycle. Along with it, he suggested the presence of a major cycle composed sometimes of two and occasionally of three minor 40-month cycles. These major cycles are merely aggregates of the minor cycles, culminating every second or third minor cycle in a major movement.

Nikolai D. Kondratieff, writing in 1926, suggested the existence of a much longer cycle with an average duration of approximately 50 years.[7] Using a wide range of statistical information, he concluded that these long cycles are international in scope and appear to occur at about the same time in Western Europe and the United States. He suggested that these long cycles are a part of the same dynamic process that produces the regular intermediate cycles of from 7 to 10 years' duration. Moreover, according to Kondratieff the presence of these long cycles modifies the nature of those of shorter length. During years of upswing in the long cycle, short cyclical fluctuations appear to contain more years of prosperity and fewer of depression. However, when the long cycle is in its downward phase, then a reverse situation prevails within the shorter cycles.

With respect to agriculture, Kondratieff stated that during the period of downswing of the long cycle, there are particularly severe and lengthy depressions in the farm sector. He cited, as an example the long agricultural depressions that followed the Napoleonic Wars and recurred in the 1870s and again during World War I. Kondratieff also suggested that it is during the periods of the long-cycle downswing that important discoveries and inventions affecting the techniques of production are made. Their actual *application* in business enterprise then follows as a part of the period of long-cycle upswing.[8]

## Schumpeter's Three-Cycle Schema

Schumpeter developed a three-cycle schema including the short Kitchin cycle of some 40-months' duration, the intermediate Juglar cycle of some 9

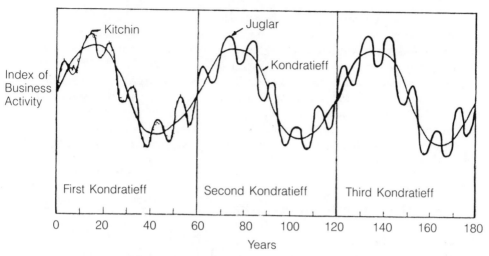

**Figure 2–3. The Three-Cycle Schema**

to 10 years in length, and the long Kondratieff cycle, which is from 48 to 60 years in duration. He maintained that each Kondratieff is composed of six Juglar cycles and that each Juglar has in it three Kitchin cycles. Thus, according to Schumpeter, the actual course of economic activity is a composite of these three types of cycles constantly interacting upon one another.

Schumpeter's three-cycle schema is illustrated in figure 2–3. It is an idealized presentation of hypothetical Kondratieff cycles extending over a period of 170 years. Around these long cycles are interwoven the intermediate Juglar 9–10-year cycle; and in turn, superimposed upon it is the short 40-month Kitchin cycle. The final Kitchin curve superimposed upon both the others is thus the *actual* curve of business activity. The positive effect of the Kondratieff upswing is apparent as succeeding Juglar and Kitchin cycles reach higher and higher peaks and recede to troughs that are never quite so low as those of preceding cycles. However, on the downswing of the Kondratieff cycle, successive peaks fail to regain the heights reached by their predecessor short-cycle peaks. Likewise, the Juglar and Kitchin troughs during this downswing phase move to successively lower and lower levels.

It has been hypothesized that the actual curve of the economic performance of the economy will be that of the Kondratieff, Juglar, and Kitchin cycles as they interact with each other. The actual turning point of any given cycle may be observed by the movements of one or the others. Thus, the beginning of the downturn from a long-cycle peak may not be evident because of the upward movement of a Juglar or Kitchin cycle at that same time. (See fig. 2–3.)

It has been suggested that the actual movements of the economy may occasionally proceed to extremely high or low levels because of the simultaneous peaking or troughing of all three of these cycles. This point of view was popular among some economists as an explanation of the severity of the Great Depression during the early 1930s.[9] The reason for the slow recovery in the 1930s was supposedly that the economy was strongly affected by a Kondratieff depression. Accordingly, there was a definite recovery movement underway from 1933 to 1937, but the peak reached in the latter year was far below the level the economy attained in 1929.

## Actual Duration of Business Cycles

Since 1930 the duration of business cycle expansions has been three years in the United States or about one year longer than in the earlier periods containing ten cycles each (see table 2–1). Each of the wartime expansions was much longer. Contractions have averaged approximately one year since 1933 but were on average twice as long before that time. Thus, a definite shift toward longer and more variable expansions and shorter and more uniform contractions is evident since the lengthy decline of 1929–1933, which is termed the Great Depression.[10] Prior to 1933, recessions were on

Table 2–1
**Average Duration of Business Cycles in the United States, 1854–1982**

| Period (Years Trough to Trough) | Number of Business Cycles Covered | Expansion (in months) Mean | S.D. | Contraction (in months) Mean | S.D. | Complete Cycle Trough to Trough (in months) Mean | S.D. |
|---|---|---|---|---|---|---|---|
| 1854–1897 | 10 | 27 | 9 | 24 | 17 | 51 | 24 |
| 1897–1933 | 10 | 23 | 10 | 20 | 10 | 43 | 10 |
| 1933–1982 | 10 | 49 | 27 | 11 | 3 | 60 | 26 |
| 1933–1982[a] | 7 | 37 | 15 | 11 | 4 | 48 | 14 |
| 1854–1982 | 30 | 33 | 20 | 18 | 12 | 51 | 22 |
| 1854–1982[a] | 25 | 27 | 11 | 19 | 13 | 46 | 16 |

Source: Adapted from Victor Zarnowitz, "Recent Work on Business Cycles in Historical Perspective: A Review of Theories and Evidence," *Journal of Economic Literature*, 23 (June 1985) : 526.

Note: Expansions are measured from troughs to peaks, contractions from peaks to troughs and the full cycles from troughs to troughs.

[a]Excluding wars.

Table 2–2

**Average Duration, Depth, and Diffusion of Thirteen Contractions, United States, 1920–1982**

| Statistic | Great Depression | Two Major Depressions | Six Severe Recessions | Four Mild Recessions |
|---|---|---|---|---|
| Average duration (months) | 43 | 16 | 12 | 10 |
| Percentage decline: | | | | |
| real GNP | −32.6 | −13.4 | −3.3 | −1.7 |
| Industrial production | −53.4 | −32.4 | −13.1 | −7.8 |
| Nonfarm employment | −31.6 | −10.6 | −3.8 | −1.7 |
| Unemployment rate: total increase (%) points | 21.7 | 9.6 | 3.8 | 2.3 |
| Nonfarm employment: percent of industries contracting | 100 | 97 | 88 | 77 |

Source: Adapted from Victor Zarnowitz, "Recent Work on Business Cycles in Historical Perspective: A Review of Theories and Evidence," *Journal of Economic Literature*, 23 (June 1985) : 528.

Note: The contractions of 8/1929–3/1933 are referred to as the Great Depression; the contractions of 1/1920–7/1921 and 5/1937–6/1938 as the major depressions. The dates of the six severe recessions are 5/1923–7/1924, 11/1948–10/1949, 7/1953–5/1954, 8/1957–4/1958, 11/1973–3/1975, and 7/1981–11/1982. The dates of the four mild recessions are 10/1926–11/1927, 4/1960–2/1961, 12/1969–11/1970, and 1/1980–7/1980.

the average only a few months shorter than expansions; since then, periods of expansion have been more than three times as long as recessions. However, the mean duration of peacetime business cycles has remained approximately four years.

The duration of business cycles shows considerable variability over time as indicated by the standard deviations presented in table 2–1. However, if some of the more unusual cycles are excluded, fairly clear central tendencies emerge. Thus, the ranges of 1½ to 3 years, 1 to 2 years, and 2½ to 5 years account, respectively, for three-fourths or more of the peacetime expansions, contractions, and complete cycles in the United States.

In the twenty years between the world wars, three major depressions occurred, including the one of 1929–1933, which was the most severe in the nation's history. Since then, no general declines of comparable magnitude have occurred in spite of the high rates of unemployment that have recently been experienced in some Western European countries and Canada. As a generalization, recessions have not only become shorter but less severe. Table 2–2 illustrates the points discussed above using a variety of business cycle indicators.

## Principal Features of Cyclical Behavior

Most industries and other economic sectors exhibit a fluctuating pattern of economic activity that generally conforms to the overall cyclical movement of the economy. However, some sectors do not. Agriculture, for example, does not conform since the level of total production is heavily dependent on the weather. Durable producer and consumer goods tend to have high conformity with the overall business cycle and exhibit wide cyclical swings in production, employment, and inventories. The amplitudes are much smaller for nondurable goods and even less for most services. Manufacturers' sales typically move with greater fluctuations than wholesalers' sales, and the latter fluctuate with greater amplitudes than retail sales. In many industries, particularly durable goods, manufacturing production is greatly influenced by advance orders that exhibit large variations followed, with variable lags, by much smaller fluctuations in outputs and shipments. The resulting changes in backlogs of unfilled orders and average delivery lags are themselves procyclical.[11] (positively correlated with the level of economic activity).

Private investment expenditures, while much smaller in the aggregate than consumer spending, have much greater cyclical variability in percentage terms. Aggregate production typically fluctuates more widely than aggregate sales, which implies a procyclical behavior of inventory investment. Business profits show very high conformity with the overall cycle and much greater amplitude of cyclical movements than wages and salaries, dividends, net interest, and rental income.

The level of industrial prices tends to have wider fluctuations than the levels of retail prices and wages. Virtually all U.S. business contractions before World War II were associated with declines in wholesale prices. (This is true for both the periods of long-term inflationary trends (1843–1864, 1896–1920) and for those of long-term deflationary trends (1864–1896 and 1920–1932). The last recession to be accompanied by a significant price deflation was that of 1948–1949. Since then, the price level has never fallen during a contraction, but in each of the seven U.S. recessions from 1953 to 1982, there was a temporary reduction in the rate of inflation. In contrast to the general price indexes for consumer and producer goods, however, prices of industrial commodities continued to show a high degree of sensitivity to business cycles, often declining even in periods of slow economic growth as well as during absolute declines in economic activity.

Narrowly and broadly defined monetary aggregates usually experience only reduced growth rates, not actual declines, in connection with ordinary recessions. Only in cycles with severe contractions do substantial downward movements interrupt the long-term major upward trends in these series. The income velocity of money (ratio of income to the stock of currency and commercial bank deposits held by the public) tends to rise in expansions and fall in business contractions.

Short-term interest rates display a procyclical movement of relatively large amplitude in comparison to their average level in each cycle. Long-term rates usually lag behind the short-term rates and have much smaller fluctuations. The relative movements in both short-term market rates and bond yields have increased significantly in the recent past as compared with their overall historical averages. At the period of business cycle peaks, short-term rates tend to come close to or exceed the long-term rates; near cyclical troughs, the former tend to be much lower than the latter.

Months before total employment, output, and real income decline, activities marking the early stages of investment activity begin to decrease. These include the formation of new business enterprises, capital investment expenditures, contracts for commercial and industrial construction, and new orders for durable goods. Investment realizations—completed construction projects, deliveries, and installations of equipment—keep increasing long after new orders for these types of investment decline. This is because work continues on the backlog of orders accumulated during the peak of the expansion. Indeed, business expenditures for plant and equipment often reach their zenith when the overall economic decline has been under way for several months. The trough or bottom of the cycle is characterized by lower levels of capacity utilization, and the delivery lags are generally shorter. Investment commitments still tend to lead overall cyclical movements, however, and expenditures coincide or lag behind fluctuations in total economic activity.

Long before the downturn in total sales, profits per unit of sales decline. Total profits (a product of profit margins times total sales) also is a leading indicator, but typically by shorter intervals. Stock prices are another leading indicator, reflecting expected changes in corporate earnings.

Labor productivity (output per hour) fluctuates procyclically around a long-term rising trend, and is usually a leading indicator of overall economic activity. Money wages often rise less than prices in recoveries (due to unemployment) and more than prices in the late stages of cyclical expansion (because of labor shortage). This combines with overall productivity changes to induce a procyclical and lagging movement in labor costs per unit of output.

Net changes in consumer installment credit and mortgage credit outstanding also exhibit procyclical behavior. So does the net change in bank loans to business, but in this case the leads tend to be shorter and more irregular. Compared with overall credit flows, the rates of growth in monetary aggregates indicate, in general, weaker cyclical patterns and fluctuations and more random variations.[12]

**Table 2–3**
**Typical Leads and Lags among Major Economic Indicators**

| *Leading* | *Roughly Coincident* | *Lagging* |
|---|---|---|
| *I. Investment in Fixed Capital and Inventories* | | |
| New building permits, housing starts, residential fixed investment | | |
| Net business formation | Production of business equipment | Backlog of capital appropriations, mfg.* |
| New capital appropriations (mfg.),* contracts and orders for plant and equipment | Machinery and equipment sales | Business expenditures for new plant and equipment* |
| Change in business inventories | | Manufacturing and trade inventories |
| *II. Consumption, Trade, Orders, and Deliveries* | | |
| New orders for consumer goods and materials | Production of consumer goods | |
| Change in unfilled orders, durable goods* | Manufacturing and trade sales | |
| Vendor performance (speed of deliveries) | | |
| Index of consumer sentiment | | |
| *III. Employment, Production, and Income* | | |
| Average workweek: overtime hours (mfg.) | | |
| Accession rate, layoff (mfg.) | Nonagricultural employment | Average duration of unemployment |
| New unemployment insurance claims | Unemployment rate | Long-term unemployment |
| Productivity (output per hour) | GNP; personal income | |
| Rate of capacity utilization (mfg., mtls.) | Industrial production, total | |
| *IV. Prices, Costs, and Profits* | | |
| Bond prices* | | |
| Stock prices* | | |
| Sensitive materials prices* | | |
| Ratio, price to unit labor cost | | |
| Profit margins | | Unit labor costs |

## Table 2–3 (continued)

| Leading | Roughly Coincident | Lagging |
|---------|--------------------|---------| 
| | *IV. Price, Costs, and Profits* | |
| Total corporate profits, cash flows | | Labor share in national net income |
| | *V. Money, Credit, and Interest* | |
| Monetary growth rates* | Velocity of money | Short-term interest rates* |
| Change in liquid assets* | Bond yields* | |
| Change in consumer credit | | Consumer credit outstanding* |
| Total private borrowing* | | Commercial and industrial loans outstanding |
| Real money supply | | |

Source: Based on indicators published monthly in *Business Conditions Digest*, Bureau of Economic Analysis, U.S. Department of Commerce.

Note: Series marked * are in nominal terms (some have the same average timing properties when deflated). All other series are in real terms (constant dollars, physical units) or related indexes and ratio numbers. The selection is based on U.S. indicators published in *Business Conditions Digest* (BCD), a monthly report by the Bureau of Economic Analysis, U.S. Department of Commerce. The timing relations among corresponding series for other countries are in many respects similar.

Abbreviations: mfg. = manufacturing; mtls. = materials.

Consumers' expectations concerning the economic and financial future also have been a leading indicator of the business cycle. Recent recessions in the United States have been characterized more often than not by downturns in consumer buying plans and actual expenditures on automobiles, housing, and related durable goods. The opposite situation has prevailed during business upturns. Residential construction commitments, such as new building permits and housing starts, have particularly long leads at peaks and often at troughs of the business cycle. In this case, the gestation periods are fairly short so that the expenditures themselves are also a leading indicator.

Changes in business inventories not only conform positively to cycles in general economic activity but also are a leading indicator of business conditions. Total manufacturing and trade inventories, on the other hand, are dominated by long trends and tend to lag behind overall cyclical movements. Inventory investment plays a very important role in short and mild cycles, whereas fluctuations in fixed investment are more important in the longer and larger cycles.

Table 2–3 provides a summary of the economic indicators that lead, are coincident with, or lag behind overall business fluctuations.

## Some International Aspects and Recent Developments

Business cycles have tended to be shorter in the United States than in Europe and England. (For example, the 1854–1938 period witnessed 21 U.S. cycles averaging 4 years and only 16 British cycles averaging 5⅓ year.[13]) After World War II ended, there was a period of reconstruction in Europe followed by rapid growth. For some time cyclical patterns in these countries were characterized by retardation of growth rather than absolute declines. The slowdowns and the intervening accelerating phases of the cycle continued to have a widespread effect on the international economy. Then overall growth slackened and the "classical" business cycles (with absolute declines in total output and employment) reappeared in Europe during the 1970s. These cycles occurred at roughly the same time in most Western European countries.

In a large economy dominated by production for domestic markets, business cycles are likely to be caused primarily by endogenous factors. They are often transmitted abroad through the movements in imports that are a positive function of production and income. In the case of small and, particularly, less-developed countries, fluctuations in exports usually have important cyclical effects. Of course, foreign influences can be critical at times for even the largest and relatively least open economy. This is well illustrated by the adverse effects on the United States of the OPEC oil price boosts in 1973–1974 and 1979–1980 expressed in increased costs and prices (leftward shifts in the aggregate supply schedule) and reduced real disposable income (hence, presumably some leftward shifts in the aggregate demand schedule). Such worldwide supply shocks, although clearly of major importance in the context of contemporary problems of productivity, growth, and development, are new and unusual events whose role in business cycles is of some importance but may on occasion be exaggerated.

The more persistent international effects come from changes in aggregate demand. Thus, the volume, prices, and value of U.S. exports show fluctuations that correspond closely to cycles in the dollar value of imports by other countries.[14] The demand changes are powerfully reinforced when the links among the major countries convert their independent cyclical tendencies into fluctuations that happen at about the same time.

These associations result not only from international trade but also from international lending and investment. The latter factor has become particularly important in the 1980s, when the integration of worldwide capital markets became a reality. Interest rates (adjusted for the anticipated exchange rate movements) are now linked internationally, and capital flows are extremely sensitive to the risk-adjusted differentials in expected rates of return.

The recent fluctuations in real economic activity show a very considerable degree of international similarity in terms of timing. This tendency presumably reflects not only the exposure to common cyclical disturbances, but also the increased economic interdependence among nations.

## Growth Cycles

During the 1960s it appeared that business contractions in Europe and Japan were being replaced by variations in overall rates of growth. At this time there was an interest in cycles that were defined as deviations from long-term growth trends rather than as absolute movements (up and down) in economic aggregates. These deviations are known as *growth cycles.* Growth cycles are sharply different from fluctuations in long-term growth rates, which reflect persistent structural changes in the overall economy.

Growth cycles also need to be clearly distinguished from business cycles. Most economic fluctuations begin with much reduced but still positive growth rates, then develop into actual declines. The high-growth phase usually coincides with the business cycle recovery and expansion while the low-growth phase occurs during late expansion and contraction. However, some slowdowns do not result in absolute declines in economic growth and subsequently move into a phase of increased expansion, not recession. Growth cycles are more numerous and more symmetrical than business cycles.

In recent U.S. experience declines in growth that have *not* led to absolute declines in aggregate economic activity occurred in 1951–1952, 1962–1964, and 1966–1967. Their adverse effects were felt primarily in areas of particular cyclical sensitivity, notably as declines in housing starts and stock prices. Unemployment ceased declining but did not rise significantly, and profits declined slightly rather than falling dramatically. Thus, the overall impact of any of these slowdowns in economic activity was definitely less than even the mildest of recent recessions.

Many of the important business cycle regularities described above are also observed within the context of growth cycles. For example, when the series that tend to lead at business cycle turns are adjusted for their own long-term trends, the resulting detrended series are generally found to be leading indicators of growth cycles. An analogous statement can be made for the roughly coincident and lagging indicators.[15]

## Fluctuations in Inventories

Changes in inventories play a major role in fluctuations in total economic activity. This has continued to be the case even in recent years, when advanced techniques of inventory control have generally resulted in a lower ratio of inventories to sales than in previous decades. The influence of inventories has been more pronounced in downturns than in expansion periods.[16] During the first postwar recession (1948–1949), the change in the rate of inventory purchases was somewhat larger than the decline in GNP. In the 1953–1954 recession, inventory adjustment was equal to about 85 percent of the change in GNP and to about 60 percent in the 1957–1958 recession. During the fourth postwar recession in (1960–1961) the change in inventory investment was more than seven times as great as the decline in GNP. In the 1969–1970 recession, which was the mildest postwar decline, inventories continued to increase, but the annual rate of accumulation was cut from $11.9 billion in the third quarter of 1969 to $2.6 billion in the fourth quarter of 1970. During the 1973–1975 recession inventory liquidation was significant. Inventories were being built up at a $27.7 billion annual rate in the peak quarter and were being reduced at a $19.0 billion annual rate in the quarter of the terminal trough.[17]

The significance of the role of inventories in the cycle is not unexpected. The acceleration principle leads to a more than proportionate change in the rate of inventory accumulation on the upswing and in the rate of liquidation in the downturn as compared to the overall change in economic activity. Speculation also leads to inventory accumulation in a recovery period and also to liquidation in a recession.

A detailed study of manufacturers' inventories was made by Moses Abramowitz, who found that fluctuations in the volume of inventories conformed well with the troughs and peaks of the cycle. There was, however, some lag in inventory movements behind those of general business. Inventory series in terms of current prices showed a lag of somewhere between 3 and 6 months, while deflated series exhibited a lag of between 6 and 12 months.[18] This lag has continued in the post–World War II recessions, but it has been somewhat shorter, especially in the earlier postwar cycles.

To understand the reasons for the fluctuations in inventories during the course of the cycle, it is necessary to analyze the factors associated with holding inventories. The most common reasons cited for holding inventories are to obtain cost savings from buying materials and supplies in larger quantities. Firms also achieve cost savings from smoothing production over a period of time, as well as providing a buffer stock against unexpected increases in demand. The benefits of holding inventories are offset in part by the costs incurred in carrying inventories. The level of inventories that a business will normally desire to hold will depend, therefore, on a balance between costs and benefits of maintaining inventories.

Two of the major costs of holding inventories are cyclically sensitive. These are interest charges and price changes or expectations of such changes. An increase in the rate of interest will increase the cost of holding inventories and thus lead to a reduction in optimum levels of inventories. A reduction in interest rates will have the reverse impact. An expected increase in prices will lead to a reduction in the relative cost of holding inventories and therefore tend to cause an increase in optimum inventory levels. An expected decline in prices will have precisely the opposite effect. Reductions in costs of holding inventories due to price rises and expected price rises are generally greater (in the early stages of expansion in business activity) than increases in costs due to higher interest rates. Thus, the net effect from the standpoint of costs leads to an increase in inventories as expansion begins. The opposite phenomenon is generally observed during business contractions, particularly in the early stages.

Variations in some of the factors that lead to cost savings from holding inventories also have a cyclical pattern. As indicated above, these include savings from buying in larger quantities and smoothing production and benefits from holding buffer stocks. In most industries cost savings are realized principally by buying goods in larger quantities. These savings include quantity discounts both in the purchase price and in transportation costs and also savings from placing and processing fewer orders.

When sales go up cyclically in an industry, costs associated with peak production will go up more than average because of longer delays in obtaining raw materials and higher labor costs due partially to more overtime work. In this situation a significant saving can be realized by accumulating inventories early in a business expansion. When few firms in an industry maintain smooth production, significant savings may be gained by an individual firm by increasing stocks early in an expansion period before prices of these items show significant increases. This is another factor that is important in explaining increases in inventory investment early in the upswing of a cycle.[19]

The result of optimal inventory policy will thus be an increase in stocks during an upswing in business that is proportionately greater than the increase in sales and a similar reduction in inventories during a downturn. These effects will be greatest when significant price rises are anticipated and when conditions are such that raw materials and parts are expected to be in limited supply. This is generally the situation in the early stages of a business upturn.

## Summary

This chapter has considered the major features of business cycles. Postwar business cycles are typically four years in length with the upward phase lasting three times as long as the downward phase. Prior to World War II the downward or contraction phase of the cycle was more severe and of longer duration.

Economic series such as new orders for durable goods, new building permits, or new unemployment insurance claims are leading indicators of economic activity. Industrial production, the velocity of money, and manufacturing and trade sales are coincident indicators; while manufacturing and trade inventories, unit labor costs and long-term unemployment are lagging indicators. The movement of these series helps to determine in which phase of the business cycle the economy is functioning.

Recessions occur at about the same time in Western Europe, Canada, and the United States. The international mobility of capital and cyclical movements in imports and exports reinforce this trend.

Inventories play a major role in cyclical movements, particularly in mild recessions. Excessive inventories and their subsequent liquidation are a major factor in the occurrence of recessions. Total inventories lag six to twelve months behind movements in overall business activity.

## Notes

1. Arthur Burns and Wesley Mitchell, *Measuring Business Cycles* (New York: National Bureau of Economic Research, 1946), p. 1.

2. Ibid.

3. Alvin Hansen, *Business Cycles and National Income*, expanded ed. (New York: W. W. Norton Co., 1964), p. 8.

4. Joseph Schumpeter, *Business Cycles*, vol. 1 (New York: McGraw Hill Book Co., 1939), pp. 207–9.

5. Clement Juglar, *Des crises commerciales et leur retour periodique en France, en Angleterre, et aux Etats-Unis* (Paris: 1862; 2d ed., 1889).

6. Joseph Kitchin, "Cycles and Trends in Economic Factors," *Review of Economic Statistics* 12, no. 1 (January 1923): 10–16.

7. Nikolai D. Kondratieff, "Die Längen Wellen der Konjunktur," *Archiv für Sozialwissenschaft und Sozialpolitik* 56, no. 3 (1926): 573–609.

8. Maurice W. Lee, Macroeconomics: *Fluctuations, Growth and Stability*, 5th ed. (Homewood, Ill.: Richard Irwin, Inc., 1971), p. 47.

9. Ibid., p. 49.

10. Victor Zarnowitz "Recent Work on Business Cycles in Historical Perspective: A Review of Theories and Evidence," *Journal of Economic Literature* 23 (June 1985): 525.

11. Ibid., p. 527.

12. Ibid., p. 529.

13. Ibid., p. 530.

14. Ilse Mintz, *Cyclical Fluctuations in the Exports of the United States Since 1879* (New York: National Bureau of Economic Research, 1967).

15. Zarnowitz, op.cit. p. 533.

16. Moses Abramovitz, *The Role of Inventories in Business Cycles* (New York: National Bureau of Economic Research, 1948); and *Manufacturers' Inventories in the Study of Economic Growth* (New York: National Bureau of Economic Research, 1959), pp. 43–44.

17. Lloyd Valentine, *Business Cycles and Forecasting*, 7th ed. (Cincinnati, Ohio: Southwestern Publishing Co., 1987), p. 95.

18. Abramovitz, op.cit., pp. 87 and 97.

19. Valentine, op.cit., p. 97.

# 3
# Theories of the Business Cycle

T his chapter appraises some of the major business cycle theories of
the past century. The classical theories are discussed first. This
presentation is followed by analysis of Keynesian and selected post-
Keynesian cycle theories, which are presented in approximate chronological
order.

Classical economists held the view that there is an inherent tendency in
the economy toward equilibrium (at full employment) and that any depar-
tures from equilibrium are temporary and will be automatically corrected in
the long run. Although most of the cycle theorists before Keynes were
trained in the classical school of thought, they did appreciate the problems
associated with cyclical instability.

## Schumpeter's Theory of Innovations and the Cycle

German-born economist Joseph Schumpeter viewed the business cycle as a
continuing process moving from phase to phase as economic development
occurs.

> Those booms consist in the carrying out of innovations in the industrial
> and commercial organism. By innovations I understand such changes of
> the combinations of the factors of production as cannot be effected by
> infinitesimal steps or variations on the margin. They consist primarily in
> changes in methods of production and transportation, or in changes in
> industrial organization, or in the production of a new article, or in the
> opening up of new markets or new sources of material. The recurring
> periods of prosperity of the cyclical movement are the form progress takes
> in capitalistic society.[1]

Thus, according to Schumpeter, these innovations are the originating
cause of cyclical fluctuations. One must understand what Schumpeter

means by an innovation, however. Innovations are not inventions. There is no evidence that inventive activity follows a cyclical pattern. Innovations are the commercial applications of new techniques or new materials or perhaps improvements in the organization of business activity. They have major economic consequences and often result in radical changes in business processes.

The cyclical upswing is a period when innovators are investing in the business application of their ideas. Expansion may begin slowly, with a few pioneers taking the greatest risk. If the results are favorable, other investors will follow along in adopting the innovations. A wave of investment occurs and will continue until the innovations begin to have their maximum effect on production. This results in a large volume of new products and perhaps in falling prices, which reduce profits and help to cause a decline in economic activity.

The lower turning point occurs when prices have fallen and costs are reduced to the point where some pioneering innovator feels justified in assuming the hazards associated with his attempt to exploit a particular innovation. It is the introduction of innovations that cause the upturn in economic activity, and the effects of the innovation that moderate the upswing and bring about its eventual reversal.

As Schumpeter indicated repeatedly, his theory may be used in conjunction with other theoretical contributions. He made use of the monetary system in his development of the business patterns that evolve once the upturn has occurred. The original innovator with more efficient production processes than his competitors may draw heavily upon the banking system for funds to aid in the commercial exploitation of his ideas. Followers will also use sources of credit, and the upswing will then ordinarily be accompanied by a considerable degree of price inflation. This in turn may lead investors to believe that expected profits will be higher than is actually the case. The success of the original innovator will attract competitors, until there is eventually a degree of overinvestment which ultimately causes the cyclical decline discussed above. The contraction occurs and the original innovations become deeply embedded within the economy although they may in time be replaced by still newer innovations.[2]

An objective evaluation of Schumpeter's theory of the cycle is extremely difficult because much of Schumpeter's contribution is based on sociological as opposed to economic factors. His hypotheses are very hard to test empirically. For example, consider his concept of the innovator as the original moving force in the initiation of the cycle. This has been compared to the "great man" approach to history. It involves issues on which there is an enormous variety of subjective opinion. In other words it is practically impossible to prove or disprove much of Schumpeter's thesis.

## The Purely Monetary Theories of the Cycle

The English economist R. G. Hawtrey was most closely associated with the purely monetary approach to the cycle.[3] According to Hawtrey, whose contributions span the first third of the twentieth century, all changes in the level of economic activity reflect variations in the flow of funds. Thus, as the money supply expands, prices rise, profits increase, and the physical volume of production is increased. When the money supply contracts, prices fall, profits decline (losses increase), business failures rise, unemployment increases, and the physical quantity of output declines. All these dimensions of the various phases of the business cycle are the result of changes in the money supply. In fact, in Hawtrey's view, fluctuations in the level of economic activity cannot occur except by changes in the flow of funds. If the money supply could be stabilized, economic fluctuations would be eliminated.

For Hawtrey, the main factor affecting the money supply is the credit mechanism. This is because the principal source of our expanded money supply is the volume of credit created by the banking system. Thus, it is the ease or tightness of credit that causes fluctuations in the money supply. The principal institution in this case is the central bank, which is in a key position to influence the flow of credit and the money supply through variations in the discount rate and open-market purchases or sales. In this way the central banks affect the reserve position of individual banks and the rates of interest they charge on loans. The overall level of interest rates tends to increase or decrease the general level of economic activity.

Taking account of the usual objection that small changes in the interest rate do not really have much effect on the overall economy, Hawtrey introduced another concept that plays a crucial role in his theory. Wholesalers and other middlemen located between the producer and the retailer are, he suggested, more sensitive to small changes in the interest rate than are producers or consumers. This is because the former need considerable credit to finance existing inventories. Any increase in interest rates will tend to cause them to curtail orders. A reduction in the costs of loanable funds will result in an increase in inventories. This will cause an increase in manufacturers' orders and a general increase in economic activity, with higher prices, expanded employment, and increased profits.

At the end of the expansion phase of the cycle, the economy is in a strained condition, with financial structures in an overextended position. Manufacturing plants are operating at capacity levels, and wholesalers are attempting to obtain increased stocks of goods for ultimate distribution to retailers. The economy is financing this high level of activity through a large volume of bank loans. The banks tighten credit as their excess reserves decline. The banks raise interest rates perhaps in response to an increase in the central bank rediscount rate. This, according to Hawtrey, is the fundamental cause of the contraction.

As the cost of loans increases, middlemen, for reasons discussed above, are quickly affected by the new level of interest rates. Since they cannot absorb this new higher level of costs, they reduce their volume of orders from the manufacturer. The latter, faced with declining volume, cuts back on his purchases of materials and lays off employees. These effects may not be experienced immediately because manufacturers have a backlog of unfilled orders that must be reduced before production declines can occur. However, new orders decline almost immediately and eventually total production falls. Throughout the economy, a decline in incomes occurs as payrolls are reduced and orders are cancelled or cut back. Some firms go out of business. Others in a relatively strong financial position have no need for borrowed funds. They repay their previous borrowings, with the result that money flows back into the banks and out of circulation. Prices fall under the impact of a general deflation. Throughout the economy there is a trend toward positions of liquidity. Loans contract, and bank reserves begin to increase. After this deflation has continued for a while, interest rates begin to decline. Because of increased deflationary pressure, interest rates are pushed to lower and lower levels. Eventually the low level of interest rates encourages some entrepreneurs to begin borrowing funds again on a limited scale.

The ultimate decline in interest rates becomes the originating cause of the turning point from contraction to expansion. The low cost of money stimulates the demand for loanable funds. Business firms begin to slowly expand the scale of their activity. Consumer incomes begin to rise, and there is an increase in effective demand for goods and services. In the early stage of economic recovery, business activity is at an extremely low level. Thus, idle resources are readily available to accommodate this expansion with little tendency for prices or costs to rise. As the expansion develops, however, excess capacity disappears and cost-price inflation occurs. Additional loans are made to accommodate not only the large volume of business but also the higher prices for which these goods are sold. Thus, the process continues until the late stages of the expansion are again reached.

Hawtrey's theory illustrates the concept of a self-generating cycle with cumulative processes of expansion and contraction. He overemphasized the purely monetary factors and exaggerated the economic importance of the wholesalers, thus ignoring the durable goods industries and other key segments of the economy.

## The Monetary Overinvestment Theories of the Cycle

Frederich Hayek was probably the leading cycle theorist of the monetary overinvestment school. Most of his works on cycle theory was written in England during the 1930s. He stressed balanced production of producer goods and consumer goods.[4] He classified output into stages of production, with the consumer goods industries representing the lowest stages. He then discussed the structure of production as the series of higher stages that build up from this lowest level. The more roundabout (capital intensive) the process of production, the more stages will be involved. Value is added as goods move from higher to lower stages.

Equilibrium exists in the economy when these different stages of the production process are in the proper relation to each other. This means the economy will be in equilibrium when there are no tendencies toward lengthening or shortening the structure of production. This would occur when the demand and supply for both consumer goods and producer goods are in equilibrium. Given that situation, there will be no tendency to increase consumption at the expense of investment or to raise investment by reducing consumption. The economy will be in a position of stability. This equilibrium may be destabilized by changes in the money supply or by a change in the relationship between savings and investment.

According to Hayek, if savings occur before investment—that is, if savings are voluntarily made out of current income, then the decrease in consumption will accommodate a proportional increase in investment spending, and there will be no tendency for prices to increase. There will be a shift of resources from the production of consumer goods to the production of producer goods, but for the economy as a whole, total employment will remain constant.

If investment takes place before saving, meaning that the banks extend credit to the capital markets through an expansion of bank loans, then a different result will follow. There will be an increase of investment without a decline in consumption, and there will be an expansion of the durable goods industries without a contraction of the consumer goods industries. These two phenomena—the increase in investment and the sustained level of consumption—cause an increase in total output. This brings about the upswing phase of the cycle, with increasing employment, rising competition for materials and other factors of production, and a general tendency for prices and costs to increase. During this cyclical expansion, the structure of production becomes more roundabout—more capital intensive.

According to Hayek, it is the net additions to the money supply that cause the excess of investment relative to consumption. This in turn produces a disequilibrium between the two principal sectors of the economy, the heavy goods and consumer goods industries. The former is expanding while the latter has a constant level of output. The disequilibrium causes a series of economic reactions, which are discussed below.

## Reactions of the Economic System

Because bank loans permit the investment industries to expand and there has been no offsetting contraction in the consumer goods industries, a net expansion of the money supply occurs. Total wages paid increase and additional funds are received by material suppliers and others who contribute to the production of goods and services. This increase in the money supply leads to general inflation. Since the consumer goods industries have not expanded, the inflationary pressure becomes particularly acute in that sector, and consumer prices rise. In effect, the new investment, which was financed by bank loans, is now compensated for by a reduced value of money being spent for consumer goods. This in effect becomes a form of forced savings.

When an expansion of investment occurs because of voluntary savings, consumers have reduced consumption to obtain investments, but according to Hayek there is no net aggregate economic expansion. Saving then occurs before investment. When the expansion of investment arises from bank loans, savings occur after investment and take the form of forced savings as prices rise. As these prices increase, the consumer goods industries experience higher rates of profit and are subsequently able to bid resources away from the investment goods industries. Ordinarily, according to Hayek, this process will continue until the structure of production has been returned to a state of balance or equilibrium, with demand and supply for both consumer and producer goods being equal. In the process of reaching this adjustment, costs will rise in the investment goods industries, profits will decline, and the increasing interest rates charged for bank loans will occur simultaneously with declining profit rates in these industries. Firms will no longer find it profitable to borrow funds, and loans will drop in response to higher interest rates. The upper turning point of the business cycle will have been reached.

Inherent in Hayek's explanation of this upper turning point of the cycle is the assumption that the economy has reached a condition of full employment.[5] This is because his upper turning point is explained in terms of an expansion in the demand for consumer goods, which initially would seem to be inconsistent with the other cycle theories as concerns the causes of a contraction. If the economy is at full employment levels, however, any expansion in one sector must come at the expense of another. An expansion of the consumer goods industries, given conditions of full employment, requires a contraction in the investment goods industries. Excess reserves decline, interest rates are increased, and borrowings fall. Then, the contraction follows an inverse pattern to that which has been presented by the upswing. Output falls, and unemployment rises. Incomes decline, and bank reserves rise as potential borrowers become unwilling to borrow at existing interest rates. The process of contraction continues until once again it becomes profitable for firms to seek loanable funds, and then expansion starts again.

This theory has indicated how processes initiated within the monetary system cause distortions in the production process. That process involves interacting responses that push the economy forward to very high levels of output and then, when the economy is unable to maintain this level of activity, it enters the contraction phase of the cycle.

There are two major criticisms of this theory. First, although forced saving may for a while produce a distortion of the structure of production in favor of the investment industries and against the consumer goods industries, this does not imply that the situation may not be automatically self correcting without a cyclical response. Much of the investment will be cost reducing and thus will lead to a greater output of consumer goods at relatively lower prices. Thus, ultimately, the consumer may be able to obtain more goods than previously, without paying more and without necessarily bidding factors of production away from the investment goods industries. Certainly, the latter has been the case for the Western economies ever since the beginning of the industrial revolution. The structure of production has lengthened, in the sense that production processes have become more capital intensive; but simultaneously the costs of many consumer goods have fallen, individual living standards have risen, and profits at all levels have remained high.

Another major criticism of monetary overinvestment theories is that they do not really explain the contraction phase of the cycle. These theories have been most useful in drawing attention to structural distortions that may develop during the cyclical upswing. There is general agreement among many theorists that a money-induced distortion between investment and consumption causes the upper turning point. The theory does not convincingly explain why, after the turning point has been reached, production methods must become less capital intensive. In addition, business cycle facts are inconsistent with this viewpoint. There is net investment even during severe depressions. The economy does not return to less capital-intensive methods of production; instead the rate of net investment falls during the period of cyclical decline.

## Nonmonetary Overinvestment Theories of the Cycle

These theories have in common with the monetary overinvestment theories the idea that the upswing is accompanied by an excessive amount of investment and that this overinvestment is the basic cause of the contraction. However, the nonmonetary overinvestment theory does not attach much importance to monetary factors. The theorists in this latter group did consider the monetary system in their explanation of the processes of cyclical fluctuation, but argued that the monetary system is a part of the response mechanism and is not one of the originating causes of the business cycle.

The money system does not cause economic fluctuations; it merely transmits them, and one must consider something more fundamental to explain the cause of the business cycle. Tugan-Baranowsky,[6] writing in 1913, introduced an example that has become widely known. He distinguished between free capital, which is today termed the supply of loanable funds, and real capital, which is the actual investment in machinery, plants, and inventories. He likened free loan capital to the steam that builds up within the cylinder of an engine. When the pressure has increased sufficiently, the piston begins to move and comes to the end of the cylinder; the steam escapes, and the piston returns to its original position. Tugan-Baranowsky's free capital plays a similar role.

As free loan capital accumulates within the economy, it builds up pressures that force the economy into a cyclical expansion. The free loan capital is thus converted into real capital (investment goods). As the expansion occurs, the economy absorbs increasing amounts of loan capital until such funds are completely utilized. Then, in the late stages of the cyclical upswing, interest rates advance rapidly. The pressure that excess supplies of free capital had formerly built up in the economy is now gone, and the expansion loses its steam (momentum). The piston begins its return course. A contraction takes place.

During the downward phase of the cycle, the greatest declines occur in the industries that supply fixed real capital. However, as these firms cancel orders for materials and reduce employment, the decline is transmitted to other parts of the economy primarily through the operation of the monetary system.

While many individuals suffer severe losses of income during the contraction, those who live on fixed incomes benefit in this situation. As prices fall during the contraction, they are able to save an increasing fraction of their income, which becomes a principal source of accumulation of free loan capital for the next expansion. Conversely, those on fixed incomes suffer declining real incomes during the expansion periods as prices rise. Eventually, they may be forced to utilize all their savings to supplement their fixed income. This contributes to the decline in the supply of loan funds in the later stages of an expansion.

Another theorist of the nonmonetary overinvestment school was German economist Arthur Spiethoff.[7] Most of his contributions to business cycle theory were made from 1901 to 1925. The core of his theoretical structure rests upon the disproportionate development of four different segments of the economy:

1. nondurable consumer goods
2. durable and semidurable consumer goods
3. durable capital goods
4. materials supplied to durable goods industries

Expansion and contraction occur through movements within and among these four divisions of the economy. During a period of depression, there is excess capacity with respect to items of capital investment such as plant and equipment. As a result, orders for durable capital goods and for the materials used for such production are at a low ebb. As the upturn begins, these heavy goods industries expand their activities and must replace old equipment and eventually plan for the expansion of capacity. This makes the primary and initial impact of a cyclical expansion greatest in the materials and durable goods–producing industries. Capital goods prices as well as profits begin to rise, thereby attracting further investment to these industries.

As the expansion continues, it results in the payment of additional wages and in general adds to the aggregate income of the employed. They increase their spending and shortages of consumer goods begin to occur. Because of increased investment demand, the possibility of satisfying the increased consumer demand is limited by the allocation of resources to the investment sector of the economy. Other investors are induced to supply capital to the durable goods producing industries. The production of consumer goods from the new investment facilities takes time, and prices and profits in the consumer goods industries increase concomitantly with the apparent shortage of consumer goods. Subsequently, as the products of this increased investment enter the market, there is a greatly increased supply of consumer goods. As more and more heavy goods plants come into production, it quickly becomes obvious that the economy is characterized by overinvestment. Returns on investment fall rapidly, prices drop, workers are laid off, and the reinforcing processes of a contraction begin to develop.

The lower turning point is reached when prices and costs have fallen sufficiently to make renewed investment attractive to those who have savings available. However, Spiethoff suggested that the real business cycle upturn may not actually occur unless some outside stimulant such as new inventions, favorable crop reports, or some other factor that reverses the pessimistic psychology, takes place at a propitious moment.

Gustav Cassel, most of whose work on cycles was published between the two world wars, another nonmonetary overinvestment theorist, was of German nationality. He developed a cycle theory similar to Spiethoff's.[8] He did not agree with Spiethoff that the basic cause of the upper turning point is an excess of investment compared to consumption. Rather, he suggested that investment should be viewed in terms of its relationship to the amount of savings available in the economy. Investment in the late stages of an upswing is hampered by the limited supply of savings. There is a sharp upward movement in the rate of interest, investment projects are postponed or cancelled, and a decline in investment occurs. Cassel would have agreed with Spiethoff that these late stages of the expansion are accompanied by a large increase in the production of consumer goods. It was Cassel's position, however, that this increased production caused individuals to spend more of their incomes on consumption, thereby reducing the supply of savings. Thus, according to Cassel, it is the disparity between savings and investment that causes the downturn.

These theorists connected the excessive level of investment to the upper turning point. Some have stressed that this investment is excessive in relation to the amount of consumption, but others have viewed it as too large for the amount of saving actually available. The cause of the lower turning point is not well explained by this theory but would appear to focus on inadequate investment in relation either to the needs of consumers or with respect to the supply of savings, so that interest rates become low enough to make the use of bank credit attractive. This aspect of the theory seems very similar to the monetary overinvestment theories discussed above.

## Keynes' Theory of the Cycle

The events of the 1930s convinced many that the course of the economy is not merely cyclical but prone to long-term severe depressions. The instability of profits, investment, and credit attracted renewed attention from business cycle theorists. Among these was the English economist John Maynard Keynes, whose contributions to business cycles and macroeconomic theory remain profoundly influential.

The general proposition presented in the Keynes' *General Theory of Employment Interest and Money*, first published in England in 1936, is as follows: "The recession of Boom and Slump can be described and analyzed in terms of the fluctuations of the marginal efficiency of capital relative to the rate of interest."[9] Keynes defined the marginal efficiency of capital as

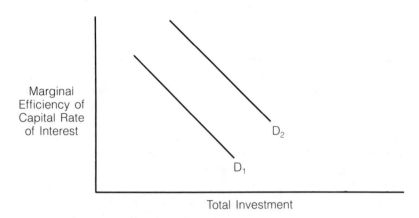

**Figure 3–1. The Marginal Efficiency of Capital**

being equal to that rate of discount that would equate the expected returns from a capital asset to its supply price.

Keynes argued that the business cycle is primarily due to a cyclical change in the marginal efficiency of capital, though complicated (and often aggravated) by variations, induced by the cycle itself, in the state of liquidity preference and in the propensity to consume. The *associated* changes serve to intensify cyclical fluctuations; but the cycle itself is basically caused by fluctuations in the marginal efficiency of capital.

A change in the marginal efficiency of capital may result from *moving down on the schedule* as a result of additional investment; or it may result from a *shift* in the schedule. According to Keynes, both play highly significant roles in terms of cyclical movements.

Let us first consider the downward movement on the marginal efficiency of capital schedule (see fig. 3–1). If we assume the schedule as given, every additional increment of investment made during the boom years means a movement to a lower point on the schedule $(D_1)$. This means the marginal efficiency of capital is pushed lower and lower by the process of investment. Further investment would cease when the marginal efficiency of investment fell as low as the prevailing rate of interest.

Movement *down* the marginal efficiency of capital schedule during the boom was described by Keynes as follows, (using as an example the U.S. economy in the years just preceding 1929): "Net investment during the previous five years had been, indeed, on so enormous a scale in the aggregate that the prospective yield of further additions was, coolly considered, falling rapidly."[10] The boom dies a natural death, since the very process of investment progressively lowers the marginal efficiency of capital.[11]

A more dynamic, and also more realistic, consideration of the above would involve combining a movement *down* the schedule with a *shift* in the schedule $(D_2)$; the net effect then would be a progressive decline in the marginal efficiency of capital. As the boom progresses, two facts become apparent, namely the increasing supply of capital goods[12] and their rising costs of production. Both of these result in a reduction in the marginal efficiency of capital. Yet the later stages of a boom are often characterized by optimistic expectations that exceed a "reasonable estimate of the future yield of capital assets."[13] These expectations are high enough to offset the rising costs of capital goods and probably also the increase in interest rates. Doubts arise with respect to the expected yield as the total stock of newly produced durable goods steadily increases. When disillusion occurs it may come suddenly and with great impact. The subsequent decline in the marginal efficiency of capital (violent downward shift in the volatile schedule) causes a sharp increase in liquidity preference. Thus, the fall in the marginal efficiency schedule tends to be associated with a rise in the rate of interest, and this *aggravates* the decline in investment. The ultimate cause of the downturn according to Keynes, however, is the fall in the marginal efficiency of capital, which may be very difficult to reverse: "Later on, a decline in the rate of interest will be a great aid to recovery and, probably, a necessary condition of it. But for the moment, the collapse in the marginal efficiency of capital may be so complete that no practicable reduction in the rate of interest will be enough."[14] This, according to Keynes, is what makes some contractions last a long time. It is difficult to increase the marginal efficiency of capital, since it is affected a great deal by psychological factors. It is the "return of confidence" that is so difficult to control.

It needs to be stressed (which Keynes did not) that once the *correct* amount of investment has been made, in relation to the prevailing level of technology and population growth, no further investment would, for the time being, be justified. The boom would cease, even though there were no errors of judgement, once the "backlog" of capital requirements was eliminated. It does not require "overinvestment" to cause the boom to end.[15]

Sporadic rates of growth of capital formation are all that is needed to produce business cycles, even if the actual stock of capital never exceeds what is justified. Cyclical fluctuations will result from occasional surges of growth, and such growth impulses need not be based on mistakes, though if errors of optimism and pessimism do occur, induced by the cycle itself, the cycle will be intensified.

## The Acceleration Principle

Both the monetary and nonmonetary overinvestment theories, as well as Schumpeter's theory of innovations, maintain that investment is the initiat-

Table 3–1

Changes in the Demand for Producer Goods Resulting from Changes in Consumer Goods Demand

| Period | Commodity Demand | Equipment Stock (Beginning of Period) | Demand for Equipment for Replacement | Demand for New Equipment (Net Investment) | Total Demand for Equipment (Gross Investment) |
|--------|------------------|---------------------------------------|--------------------------------------|-------------------------------------------|-----------------------------------------------|
| 1 | 2,000 | 200 | 20 | 0 | 20 |
| 2 | 2,200 | 200 | 20 | 20 | 40 |
| 3 | 2,300 | 220 | 22 | 10 | 32 |
| 4 | 2,300 | 230 | 23 | 0 | 23 |
| 5 | 2,000 | 230 | 23 | −30 | −7 |

Source: Hypothetical data.

Note: Figures are based on the following assumptions:
1. Commodity demand figures are arbitrarily selected.
2. One piece of equipment produces at the rate of 10 units of the commodity per period.
3. The equipment has a life of 10 periods; that is, its depreciation rate is 10 percent per year. In reality, the assumption is that in its lifetime, the equipment is capable of producing 100 units of the commodity.
4. No depreciation occurs in the year in which equipment is added.

ing factor as regards the business cycle. An alternative view of the cycle maintains that changes in consumer demand play a major role in economic fluctuations. According to this latter position, variations in consumer expenditures can lead to a cyclical pattern of economic activity because slight changes in the demand for consumer goods can produce much larger fluctuations in the demand for investment goods. This concept, known as the *acceleration principle*, has been used by a number of theorists as part of their explanation of cyclical economic fluctuations.

The acceleration principle states that variations in the absolute rate of change in the demand for and production of finished goods and services tends to cause much larger fluctuations in the demand for the capital goods that are needed for the production of the former.[16] This principle applies not only to finished consumer goods but to all intermediate goods with respect to their earlier stages of production. It also relates to changes in demand resulting from factors other than fluctuations in final demand, such as changes in technology necessitating additional machinery to produce a given level of output. The acceleration principle can also be applied to a degree in the production of durable and semidurable consumer goods.

The relationship in the case of producer durable goods can be illustrated by means of a hypothetical example (illustrated in table 3–1). Suppose that in a given economy 2,000 units of consumer goods are produced in a year and that it takes 200 units of producer durable equipment to manufacture the consumer goods. If the capital equipment lasts ten years, there is an average demand for 20 units of equipment each year to replace those that are wearing out in order to keep the stock of equipment constant.

Let us also assume that there is an increase of 10 percent in the demand for this particular consumer good so that 2,200 units are now desired by consumers. To produce these additional 200 units, it will be necessary to have 20 more units of equipment. Although this equipment will be useful for a period of ten years, it is needed immediately. As a result, there is now a demand for 40 units of equipment, the 20 needed for replacement and the 20 additional units required because of increased consumer demand. Thus, an increase of 10 percent in the demand for consumer goods has been magnified into an increase of 100 percent in the demand for producer goods.

The magnitude of this acceleration in the derived demand for capital goods depends upon the life of the capital equipment. If the machines in our example lasted only 5 years, there would be a normal replacement demand of 40 per year. In this case, a 10 percent increase in the demand for consumer goods would result in a 50 percent increase in the demand for producer goods since 20 additional machines would be needed and 40 were being produced prior to the increased demand for consumer goods. However, if the machines lasted 20 years, the normal replacement demand would be only 10 per year and the 10 percent increase in the demand for consumer goods would lead to a 200 percent increase in the demand for producer equipment.

It is possible for the demand for new equipment to decline even while the demand for consumer goods is still increasing. If the demand for the consumer goods increases from 2,000 to 2,200 units, the demand for equipment increases by 20, or 100 percent as indicated above. If the demand for consumer goods continues to increase to 2,300 units, the total demand for equipment would decline to 32 units, a reduction of 20 percent. If in the next period the demand for the commodity remains constant (2,300 units), the only equipment demand is for replacement and, as a result, demand falls even more.

Thus, increases in the absolute rate of change in demand for consumer goods when an industry is at or near capacity will lead to an accelerated derived demand for producer goods. This demand will decline sharply as the rate of increase falls, however.

The acceleration principle is a concept that partially explains the sharp increase in demand during the expansion phase of the cycle. It is especially significant in a highly developed economy in which large amounts of capital equipment are being utilized, with much of the equipment having a long economic life. As indicated above, the longer the life of the equipment, the greater the degree of acceleration due to derived demand. Since some of the new capital equipment is financed out of credit expansion, the additional credit intensifies the upswing. The acceleration in demand for durable goods and inventories also offers a further explanation of the factors leading to the cumulative nature of the business expansion.

The acceleration principle also provides insight regarding the cause of the downturn. Instead of being due solely to a shortage of money or capital goods, the contraction may occur simply because the rate of increase in the demand for consumer goods has slowed down, thus reducing the demand for new equipment and leading to unemployment in the producer goods industries. This further reduces the demand for consumer goods, causing an additional reduction in demand for producer goods.

## The Multiplier and the Cycle

In addition to the accelerator, the multiplier has an important role in modern theories of the cycle. While the investment multiplier relates the magnified effect of an increment of investment upon income, it is not true that the multiplier process operates only through exogenous increases or decreases in investment. An upward shift of the consumption function (that is, a general increase in the propensity to consume) will raise income by a magnified amount, in exactly the same manner as an increase in investment.[17]

An increase in investment raises income in the capital goods industries and this in turn increases the spending on consumer goods. Moreover, an increase in consumption will likewise raise income in the consumer goods industries. This will similarly lead to an increase in consumer expenditures and thus raise income by an amount greater than the initial increase in spending.

Changes in income expectations are an almost certain result of the magnified impact of additional investment, and these expectations lead to changes in the propensity to consume and therefore in the multiplier. Variations in price expectations are a likely result of new investment expenditures. Thus, changes in expected prices do cause shifts in the consumption function. Improved employment prospects are a likely result of increased investment expenditures, and such optimistic expectations will tend to cause a modification in the consumption-saving pattern. Past income experience is also one of the reasons for a change in the marginal propensity to consume.[18]

When the above factors are considered, it is unlikely that the marginal propensity to consume will remain constant during a time when increased investment has led to higher levels of income through the impact of the

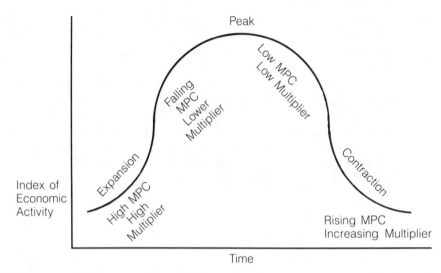

**Figure 3–2. Schematic Illustration of Cyclical Variation in Multiplier and Marginal Propensity to Consume (MPC)**

multiplier. Figure 3–2 presents an illustration of the way in which the marginal propensity to consume varies over the course of the business cycle.

Proceeding from the trough of the business cycle, the recipients of additional increments of income are using the money primarily for additional consumption; the marginal propensity to consume and the multiplier are relatively high. As the expansion continues, individuals begin to allocate some additional income to saving; and both the marginal propensity to consume and the multiplier decline. Near the peak of the business cycle, there is an attempt to increase saving; the marginal propensity to consume declines considerably and the cyclical contraction occurs. Eventually the marginal propensity to consume begins to rise again and this phenomena is associated with a rising value of the multiplier.

Until now, the major emphasis has been on personal saving as opposed to business saving. The latter is also important because of possible cyclical variation in the marginal propensity to consume. Corporate profits are cyclically volatile, and retained earnings vary in a manner consistent with the movements in total corporate profits but with fluctuations of greater magnitude than those of corporate profits.[19]

The above discussion implies that there will be a significant procyclical movement of the saving-income ratio and a strong contracyclical variation in the consumption-income relation. This will in turn tend to have a stabilizing effect upon the fluctuations in the overall economy. The more that savings (rather than consumption) vary with respect to changes in national

Table 3–2
**Multiplier and Accelerator Interrelation**

| Period | Govern-mental Expendi-ture | Consumption Induced by Previous Expenditure (Marginal Propensity to Consume = 0.5) | Investment Induced by Increase in Consumption (Accelerator = 1.0) | Total Income |
|--------|------|-----------|------------|------------|
| 1  | 1.00 | —         | —          | 1.00     |
| 2  | 1.00 | 0.50      | 0.50       | 2.00     |
| 3  | 1.00 | 1.00      | 0.50       | 2.50     |
| 4  | 1.00 | 1.25      | 0.25       | 2.50     |
| 5  | 1.00 | 1.25      | 0.00       | 2.25     |
| 6  | 1.00 | 1.125     | −0.125     | 1.875    |
| 7  | 1.00 | 1.00      | −0.125     | 1.875    |
| 8  | 1.00 | 0.9375    | −0.625     | 1.875    |
| 9  | 1.00 | 0.9375    | 0.00       | 1.9375   |
| 10 | 1.00 | 0.96875   | 0.03125    | 2.00     |
| 11 | 1.00 | 1.00      | 0.03125    | 2.03125  |
| 12 | 1.00 | 1.015625  | 0.00       | 2.015625 |
| 13 | 1.00 | 1.0078125 | −0.0078125 | 2.00     |

Source: Adapted from Paul A. Samuelson, "Interactions between the Multiplier Analysis and the Principle of Acceleration," in *Readings in Business Cycle Theory* (Philadelphia: Blakiston Co., 1944), p. 262.

income, the less will be the total cyclical impact on expenditures and total production.

## Interaction Between Multiplier and Accelerator

The multiplier and accelerator tend naturally to reinforce each other, moving the economy to very high levels or, in the opposite case plunging the economy into severe recession or depression.

An increase in investment may cause an expansion in consumption, as determined by the value of the multiplier; and the subsequent increase in consumption may, in turn, result in new investment. Theoretically the interrelation could lead the economy to an explosive expansion or contraction, depending upon the values of the multiplier and accelerator. The classic paper on this interrelationship is Samuelson's, from which table 3–2 is adapted.[20]

Table 3–2 assumes a marginal propensity to consume of 0.5, meaning that one half of any additional income is spent on consumer goods. It is further assumed that there is a one-period lag, so that the induced consumption takes place one period after the appearance of the additional

Table 3–3
Variations in Total Income Effect Using Different Multipliers and Accelerators

| Period | M = 0.5<br>A = 1.0 | M = 0.5<br>M = 0.0 | M = 0.5<br>A = 2.0 | M = 0.6<br>A = 2.0 | M = 0.8<br>A = 4.0 |
|---|---|---|---|---|---|
| 1 | 1.00 | 1.00 | 1.00 | 1.00 | 1.00 |
| 2 | 2.00 | 1.50 | 2.50 | 2.80 | 5.00 |
| 3 | 2.50 | 1.85 | 3.75 | 4.84 | 17.80 |
| 4 | 2.50 | 1.875 | 4.125 | 6.352 | 56.20 |
| 5 | 2.25 | 1.9275 | 3.4375 | 6.6256 | 169.84 |
| 6 | 2.00 | 1.9688 | 2.0313 | 5.3037 | 500.52 |
| 7 | 1.875 | 1.9844 | 0.9141 | 2.5959 | 1,459.592 |
| 8 | 1.875 | 1.9922 | −0.1172 | −0.6918 | 4,227.704 |
| 9 | 1.9375 | 1.9961 | 0.2148 | −3.3603 | 12,241.1216 |

Source: Adapted from Paul A. Samuelson, "Interactions between the Multiplier Analysis and the Principle of Acceleration," in *Readings in Business Cycle Theory* (Philadelphia: Blakiston Co., 1944), p. 266.

income. With respect to the accelerator, it is assumed that the increase in consumption will induce new investment equal to the difference between consumption of the previous period and that of the present period. Successive increments of new expenditure of 1.00 amount are added each period in the form of government spending.

In period 1, the first 1.00 of government spending occurs; and this produces 0.50 of new consumption, which, in turn, being 0.50 above the previous level of consumption, induces the same amount of new investment; and aggregate income now increases to 2.00. The cyclical pattern may be traced in the column of total aggregate income, where a peak is reached in periods 3–4, a trough in periods 7–8, and another peak in periods 11–12.

Quite different results were demonstrated by Samuelson when he altered the values of the multiplier and the accelerator. This is shown in table 3–3, where the components of income are omitted and only the final column of total aggregate income is presented for the several multiplier and accelerator values indicated. The first column is taken from table 3–2. The second column shows an increase in income (at a decreasing rate) due only to the multiplier, since the accelerator is given a zero value. Column 3 shows the same multiplier with the accelerator raised to a value of 2.0; this interaction produces a cycle effect, which was not present in the previous case. Column 4 has the same value for the accelerator but increases the marginal propensity to consume to 0.6; and in this case, cycles of considerably greater amplitude are generated. When both the multiplier and accelerator have high coefficients, as in the final column, there are no cyclical fluctuations, but total aggregate income expands explosively.

These examples illustrate some of the range of possibilities that can occur in the interaction between the multiplier and the accelerator. Since the change in total aggregate income could itself tend to produce variations in the values of the accelerator and multiplier, the constancy implicit in each of these columns of table 3–3 is unrealistic. In addition, the multiplier accelerator combinations in columns 3 and 4 result in negative economic output, which is an absurd result.

## Hick's Model of Growth and Economic Fluctuations

The work of J. R. Hicks represents a major advance in business cycle theory. His book, *A Contribution to the Theory of the Trade Cycle*, provides a powerful analysis of the interaction of economic growth and business cycles.[21]

The Hicksian model relies upon three formal relationships: (1) the multiplier, (2) the accelerator, and (3) the concept of a warranted rate of growth around which the multiplier and accelerator bring about a cyclical pattern of economic activity.

Hicks's multiplier is presented as a lagged relationship, so that today's consumption is treated as a function of yesterday's income: $C_t = pY_{t-1}$. Similarly, saving is a function of income obtained in a previous period. Hick's multiplier thus acts as a damped expansive factor on the upswing and a lagged force during the downswing of the cycle.

The second basis of Hicks's cycle theory is the acceleration principle. For this purpose, he distinguishes between autonomous and induced investment. Autonomous investment occurs independently of the growth of the economy. It consists of investment expenditures made to replace deteriorated stocks or capital used up in the production process. Autonomous investment is therefore a function of the current level of output: $I_a = gY_t$.

Induced investment is a function of the *change* in the level of output, a function of the growth rate of the economy. An increase in output from one period to the next produces an upswing in investment, which will then interact through the multiplier until its effects have been fully realized.

Hick's differentiation of autonomous and induced investment is an important feature of his theory. As mentioned previously, autonomous investment is a function of total output in the current period. This investment is continuous and stands in a fixed ratio to output. Induced investment varies in proportion to the *rate of change* in total output. In Hicks' theory this is the accelerator, and it is used with a lag, as in the case of the multiplier. Hicks suggested that a given rate of change in total output will induce a given amount of additional new investment in the subsequent period. Moreover, just as he assumed a fixed consumption function for purposes of the multiplier, he also assumed a fixed ratio of investment to output growth, in both cases with a fixed lag. His model, in other words, is constructed upon the basis of a fixed consumption function and a fixed investment function.

Although both consumption and investment functions are fixed throughout the cycle, only the consumption function (and the multiplier derived from it) operate throughout all portions of the cycle. The accelerator becomes inoperative during certain phases.

During the expansion, Hicks's accelerator and multiplier operate to produce the sort of interacting effect discussed previously. The expansion of investment operates through the multiplier and causes an increase of consumption and income. This increase in expenditures, working through the accelerator, then induces additional investment. At the same time, autonomous investment continues steadily at a fixed ratio to total output. Both the multiplier and accelerator are lagged in Hick's model, so that current consumption and investment expenditures are a function of previous income levels and changes in income.

Hicks introduced a realistic concept relating to the downswing, that was missing from earlier models. He recognized the fact that after the upper turning point has been reached, there will be excess capacity. Thus, investment will fall, and each decline in investment, working through the multiplier, will produce additional drops in income and consumption expenditures. While during the expansion phase of the cycle, increases in consumption will induce proportionally related increases in investment, during the downswing this accelerator becomes inoperative. This is because decreases in aggregate income and consumption can account for only part of the decline in investment since investment cannot become negative, and disinvestment can be no larger than the failure to offset depreciation and the amount of capital stocks used up. Thus, according to Hicks, the upswing is largely the result of an interaction between fixed investment and the consumption function, or between the accelerator and the multiplier. The downswing is largely the product of the workings of the multiplier, with the accelerator partially inoperative.

Although the above explains expansion and contraction, it does not address the matter of the cause of business cycle turning points. What turns an expansion into a contraction, and what reverses the course of a downswing? According to Hicks, the lower turning point is largely explained by the functioning of autonomous investment. During the contraction, as discussed above, induced investment is at negative levels. The economy continues to produce goods and services, but in decreasing amounts. Since it is producing some quantity of output, it is drawing down inventories and wearing out plant and equipment. The amount of spending necessary to replace this amount of "depreciation" is what Hicks termed autonomous investment. Disinvestment during the downswing may reach magnitudes equal to autonomous investment; but as the decline continues, a point is finally reached when inventories are depleted and equipment must be replaced. Thus, the quantity of autonomous investment that, according to Hicks, stands in fixed ratio to total output serves as a stabilizing factor for the economy during the downswing. At some point during the contraction, the amount of disinvestment becomes less than the amount of autonomous investment, and a net expenditure for investment occurs. At this point, the lower turning point of the cycle has been reached. There is an increase in aggregate income. The increment of net investment produces, through the operation of the multiplier, a magnified addition to income and consumption expenditures, which, in turn, induce a further net investment expenditure. Thus, the upturn gains momentum, sustained by the interaction of the multiplier and accelerator, as discussed above.[22]

The upper turning point, according to Hicks, is more difficult to explain. Hicks differentiates between two types of business cycle "endings." A cycle has a "strong" ending when the upturn reaches the full employment of resources. This is a limit imposed by population, technology, the stock of capital, and other inputs. Thus, for a strong cycle ending, the peak occurs when the upward movement powered by the interacting multiplier and accelerator carries the economy to the level of the production ceiling.

A weak cycle ending and upper turning point occur whenever the interaction of the multiplier and accelerator is not of sufficient strength to carry the economy to the level of the production ceiling (full employment). Cycles with weak endings Hicks terms "free" cycles as compared to those that are limited by the production ceiling, which he calls "constrained" cycles.

Hick's model assumes that both investment and consumption functions are constant throughout the cycle, with constant coefficients for both the accelerator and multiplier. The constant multiplier is, of course, derived from a constant marginal propensity to consume out of income. As noted previously, however, there seems to be no reason to believe that a constant proportion of income would be devoted to consumption during all phases of the cycle. Moreover, there are also changes in the distribution of income over the course of the cycle; there are price movements and changed expectations as to future income. Each of these might be expected to cause variations in the marginal propensity to consume over the course of the business cycle. Thus, Hicks's use of a constant multiplier over all phases of the cycle seems inappropriate.

The fixed value accelerator is also a controversial aspect of Hick's model. There is clearly a relationship between changes in income and consumer spending, and the quantity of capital facilities. There are great variations, however, in the ratio of capital to output as between different sectors of the economy. Moreover, there are differences in the gestation period for different types of investment expenditures. Plans to expand inventories can be realized quickly, but the construction of a major plant takes years. Some upturns may be characterized by expansion in the durable goods industries; in other cases the dominant growth sector may be consumer goods or agriculture. Since the expansion in output may induce a wide variety of investment reactions, the assumed constancy of the accelerator is very questionable.

No explanation that overlooks the actual process by which investments are made can adequately account for the rise and fall of investment activity. In our modern capital-using economy, most investment decisions are made by individual businessmen. These decisions are not based upon precise mathematical formulas in which investment is a precise function of output. The productive life of a major capital investment, which may extend for twenty-five or fifty years, makes any precise relationship between output and investment highly suspect.

There have been a limited number of attempts to make statistical tests of various aspects of Hicks's cycle theory. Tinbergen concluded that there was practically no consistent lag between fluctuations in the production of investment goods and consumer goods, which would be necessary to support the accelerator principle. Other studies have also failed to produce support for the idea of a fixed accelerator, although, the principle is not one that can be easily verified or proven wrong.[23]

## The Modern Monetary Theory

The monetary theory of the business cycle once again acquired importance after the depression and early postwar era, a period when most economists felt that the money supply was not a major consideration in explaining the cycle. The majority of economists today believe that monetary factors play a significant role in economic fluctuations. Debate revolves around such issues as the relative importance of monetary factors and the way in which money stock changes impact on variation in other economic magnitudes.

A great amount of empirical work has been done in recent years on the role of monetary issues in the business cycle. The evidence of close correspondence between the money stock and general economic activity is impressive. Friedman and Schwartz found that over a period of almost one hundred years, the stock of money generally increased during both expansion and contraction phases of the business cycle.[24] During the most severe business downturns, however, the stock of money did actually decline. They found that not only were the rates of change in the money stock closely associated with general business conditions, but that the magnitude of the rate of change in money stock and the cyclical movements in business were closely correlated.

As indicated in chapter 2, the money supply series normally is a leading indicator of the business cycle, but the length of the lead varies. The variability in the presumed response of the economy to changes in the quantity of money has not been adequately explained.

It appears that *changes* in money growth, rather than the rate of growth itself, are correlated with the business cycle. Since 1907—the first year for which monthly money stock data are available—there has never been a recession when money growth was rising. Historically, money growth has usually declined before the beginning of a recession, and the lower rate of money growth has usually extended into the contraction. Less frequently, money growth has declined about the time a recession has begun, and the lower growth has continued during the recession. Money growth has typically stabilized, or risen, before a recession has ended and a recovery begun. These relationships are illustrated in figure 3–3, which shows money growth from the same quarter a year earlier and shaded areas indicating recessions.

Fluctuations in money growth have been related in part to the emphasis on interest rates in the conduct of monetary policy. When the economy is weak, credit demands and interest rates tend to decline. Under these circumstances, a decline in money growth is not appropriate; money growth should be maintained and interest rates permitted to fall more rapidly to provide support for a weakening economy. Similarly, if interest rates are held down in the face of unexpected strength in the economy, money growth may rise, contributing to the development of inflation. Steady money growth tends to act as an automatic stabilizer. Thus, interest rates rise automatically when the economy strengthens and fall when the economy weakens.

## Models of Financial Instability

Speculative excesses or "manias" have attracted the attention of contemporaries and economic historians at least since the Dutch Tulip Bubble of 1625–1637. Financed by credit expansion and characterized by "overtrading" in real or financial assets such as gold, land, or securities, they have been associated with more than two dozen major booms in business activity, often involving many countries.[25] Historically, they tended to be followed by "panics," that is, distress selling of the same assets to reacquire money and repay debt, and crashes in the prices of the now illiquid objects of the speculation. The resulting financial crises accompanied or aggravated downturns in the business cycle.

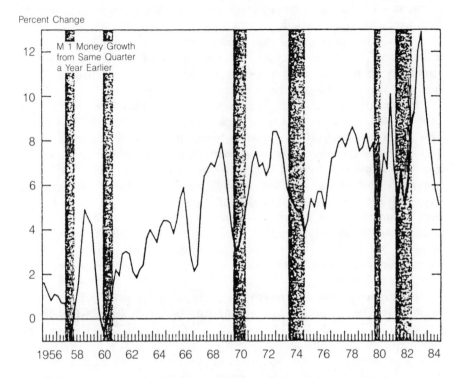

Percent Change

**Figure 3–3. Money Growth and the Business Cycle**
Source: Board of Governors of the Federal Reserve System (except as noted).
Note: Shaded areas indicate recessions (peak to trough) as defined by the National Bureau of
Economic Research.

Mild financial crises of recent U.S. history, called "credit crunches," are associated primarily with reduced availability of credit, not high interest rates per se.[26] Credit rationing by banks is linked to imperfect information about the borrowers' default risk.[27] When banks refuse to renew outstanding loans, high-risk borrowers and many small firms are unable to secure credit elsewhere and are forced to curtail investment and perhaps current operations. The retrenchment may or may not be caused by restrictive open-market policies of the central bank. Under a fractional banking system loans and deposits are closely associated so one cannot use data on the aggregates to differentiate between the "credit" hypothesis and the "money supply" hypothesis of a downturn.[28]

Hyman Minsky argues that long periods of prosperity interrupted only by mild recessions or slowdowns breed overconfidence, excessive short-term financing by banks of long-term business projects, investment booms interacting with stock market booms, growing indebtedness, and illiquidity. Innovative practices and new financial instruments are used to increase the availability of investment funds. The supply of money becomes at some point inelastic as uncertainty grows and banks increasingly retrench (or monetary authorities act to constrain inflation). The demand for credit to finance planned and existing investment projects nevertheless continues to rise. It takes sharp increases in interest rates and declines in the present value of expected net returns on capital assets to check and reverse the expansion in new investment. Business cash flows and profits decline and eventually so do total sales, output, and employment. The resulting losses force many industrial concerns and financial intermediaries into refinancing of debt and liquidation of assets to raise funds. Many businesses experience retrenchment. Some go out of business. When a sufficiently large number of these firms experience cash flow difficulties, a financial crisis must occur. This can only be averted by central bank intervention injecting sufficient money into the system to prevent large bank defaults and business failures. If a crisis is averted and stimulative monetary and fiscal policies continue, a mild recession may ensue but another inflationary and eventually destabilizing investment boom will soon follow.[29]

This is a disequilibrium theory with strong endogenous elements. The originating factors are real, but monetary and credit changes have much to do with the development of the cycle and are primarily responsible for its worst features. Minsky's hypothesis predicts the recurrence of financial crises and business depressions and is thus controversial. It is difficult to test (in part because financial crises and depressions are rare and complex events). In general terms, however, the account provided by Minsky tends to be consistent with the history of speculative investment booms, financial crises, and deep depressions in the United States.[30]

## Summary

The six decades from the 1870s to 1930s saw the development of a number of new approaches to explaining the business cycle, including monetary, monetary overinvestment, and nonmonetary overinvestment theories. These theories have much in common; their differences appear to center more on the issue of originating causes than on the responses of the economic system during the various phases of the cycle. Mainly endogenous in focus, they concentrate on internal dynamics of the economic system. These early theorists believed that cyclical movements have a strong tendency to persist even where there are no outstanding exogenous influences at work that can plausibly be held responsible.

Although these theorists were classical economists, they generally appreciated the problem of economic instability. The recurrent phases of widespread unemployment and idle industrial capacity did (and still do) present a major challenge to the classical doctrine. The latter presupposes that the economy is always in or at least tending close to full employment.

The 1930s convinced many that the course of the economy is not merely cyclical but depression prone. The instability of profits, investment, and credit attracted renewed attention. In the 1940s and 1950s there was a rise of interest in the dynamics of multiplier-accelerator interaction, yielding highly aggregative and purely endogenous models of the cycle. The monetary, financial, and expectational aspects of the cycle were largely neglected. Soon strong reactions developed against this narrow view of cyclical fluctuations.

One reaction against theories of endogenous instability was monetarism. It criticized the Keynesian model of aggregate demand as well as earlier models with unstable credit-investment interactions. Fluctuations in monetary growth were made primarily responsible for disturbing the basically stable private economy and creating "business cycles."

Minsky has recently emphasized the role of credit availability as a major factor in business cycles. Speculative excesses and "credit crunches" are seen to be capable of causing severe contractions.

## Notes

1. Joseph Schumpeter, "The Explanation of the Business Cycle," *Economica* 7, no. 21 (December 1927): 295.

2. Maurice Lee, *Macroeconomics: Fluctuations, Growth and Stability*, 5th ed. (Homewood, Ill.: Richard Irwin, Inc., 1971), p. 240.

3. R. G. Hawtrey, *Good and Bad Trade* (London: Constable & Co. Ltd., 1913); and *Capital and Employment* (London: Longman, Green and Co., Ltd., 1937).

4. Friedrich Hayek, *Monetary Theory and the Trade Cycle* (New York: Harcourt, Brace & Co., 1933); and *Profits Interest and Investment* (London: George Routledge & Sons Ltd., 1939).

5. Lee, op.cit., p. 225.

6. Michel Tugan-Baranowsky, *Les Crises Industrielle in Angleterre* (1913).

7. Arthur Spiethoff, *Business Cycles*, International Economic Papers, no. 3 (New York: The Macmillan Co., 1953).

8. Gustav Cassel, *Theory of Social Economy* (New York: Harcourt, Brace & Co., 1923).

9. John M. Keynes, *The General Theory of Employment, Interest and Money* (New York: Harcourt, Brace & Co., 1936), p. 144.

10. Ibid.

11. Alvin Hansen, *Business Cycles and National Income*, Expanded Edition (New York: W. W. Norton, Inc., 1964), p. 338.

12. This relates to movement down the marginal efficiency of capital schedule.

13. Keynes, op.cit., p. 16.

14. Ibid., pp. 316–17.

15. Ibid., pp. 341–42.

16. Carl Dauten and Lloyd Valentine, *Business Cycles and Forecasting*, 5th ed. (Cincinnati, Ohio: South-Western Publishing Co., 1978), p. 131.

17. Hansen, op.cit., p. 171.

18. Maurice Lee, *Macroeconomics: Fluctuations, Growth and Stability*, 5th ed. (Homewood, Ill.: Richard Irwin, Inc., 1971), p. 328.

19. Ibid., p. 329.

20. Paul Samuelson, "Interactions between the Multiplier Analysis and the Principle of Acceleration," *Review of Economics and Statistics*, 21, no. 2 (May 1939): 75–78.

21. John Hicks, *A Contribution to the Theory of the Trade Cycle* (London: Oxford University Press, 1950).

22. Lee, op.cit., p. 368.

23. J. Tinbergen, "Critical Remarks on Some Business Cycle Theories," *Econometrica* 10, no. 2 (April 1942): 129–46; and Simon Kuznets, "Relation Between Capital Goods and Finished Products in the Business Cycle," *Economic Essays in Honor of Wesley Clair Mitchell* (New York: Columbia University Press, 1935), 211–67.

24. Milton Friedman and Anna Schwartz, "Money and Business Cycles," *The Review of Economics and Statistics* 45, no. 1 (supplement, February 1963): 32–64.

25. Charles Kindleberger, *Manias, Panics and Crashes: A History of Financial Crises* (New York: Basic Books, 1978), pp. 6–7.

26. Albert Wojnilower "The Central Role of Credit Crunches as Recent Financial History," *Brookings Papers on Economic Activity*, vol. 2 (1980), pp. 277–326.

27. Alan Blinder and Joseph Stiglitz, "Money Credit Constraints and Economic Activity," *American Economic Review* 73, no. 2 (May 1983): 297–302.

28. Benjamin Friedman, "The Roles of Money and Credit in Macroeconomic Analysis," in *Macroeconomics, Prices and Quantities: Essays in Memory of Arthur Okun*, ed. James Tobin (Oxford: Basil-Blackwell, 1983), pp. 161–199.

29. Hyman Minsky, *Stabilizing an Unstable Economy*, A Twentieth Century Fund Report (New Haven, Conn.: Yale University Press, 1986).

30. Kindleberger, op.cit., pp. 15–18.

# 4

# Postwar Business Cycles

T he postwar reconversion period was viewed with fear and concern
by many economists and policy makers who felt that the economy
would experience a slump. As the economy converted to peacetime
production in late 1945 and 1946, wartime controls were removed. Price
control was partially dismantled shortly after the end of the war and
completely eliminated on June 30, 1947, except for rent control in areas
experiencing housing shortages. Prices rose rapidly when controls were
lifted.

Production decreased in 1946 and employment declined slightly.[1] The
reason why production fell more rapidly than employment is that most
firms adjusted to production decreases by eliminating overtime. In 1947
production and employment again increased; the year was one of virtually
full employment of labor and capital, and consumer demand continued at a
high level. Prices moved upward during 1947 as consumer and producer
demand rose more rapidly than supply. During the second quarter of the
year there was a tendency for domestic economic activity to grow more
slowly.

As the world agricultural situation worsened, primarily because of poor
crops in 1947, the foreign demand for farm products created new upward
pressure on prices. Exports increased generally and reversed the declining
tendencies that were beginning to be felt in some economic sectors. Foreign
countries used their dollar resources so extensively that those funds were
quickly exhausted. The foreign aid program passed by Congress (the Mar-
shall Plan) kept foreign demand at a high level, but below that reached
during the second quarter of 1947.

## The 1948–1949 Recession

The economy continued to operate at close to capacity levels during most
of 1948. Wartime income tax rates were cut in the spring of 1948, and the

additional disposable income had an expansionary effect on the economy. The price level increased more slowly in 1948 than in the previous year, and the rate of increase in consumption expenditures began to slacken. Firms did not adjust immediately to this change in the rate of increase in consumer spending, and consequently businesses found themselves with excessive inventories. Toward the end of 1948 and during the first quarter of 1949, firms reduced their purchases of goods and services, and substantial inventory liquidation took place.

Primarily as a result of the decline in inventories, industrial production was reduced about 8 percent. Durable goods production fell 10 percent, but nondurable production dropped only 5 percent. Total employment declined slightly, and manufacturing employment was reduced by 9 percent. Construction activity increased throughout 1949, and expenditures on producers' durable equipment were down by only 5 percent.

One reason that the business decline was not more severe was that personal consumption expenditures remained stable and even increased slightly toward the end of 1949. This was due in part to the payment of unemployment compensation to most of the workers who were laid off and also to the demand-creating effects of lower federal income taxes, which resulted from the 1947 Revenue Act.

It became evident in the second half of 1949 that inventory liquidation had become excessive. Inventory accumulation was resumed in early 1950 and economic activity concomitantly increased. A new boom began later in the year as the Korean War and large-scale rearmament led to sharply higher demand for goods and services.

## The Korean War Period

The demand for goods arising out of the Korean War led to renewed inflationary pressures. Government deficits were not the cause of price rises in the last half of 1950, since the Treasury had a surplus of nearly $1 billion for the second half of that year. The expansion was due to a sharp increase in private spending. Consumers, remembering the shortages of World War II, spent large amounts on various types of durable and semidurable goods. Business also spent heavily for inventories and capital investment.

Given these conditions, the Federal Reserve System expanded the supply of money and credit considerably. Although the Board of Governors of the Federal Reserve System wanted to act to restrict expansion, they were prevented from doing so by obligations to support the bond market by purchasing all government securities at or above par. The Treasury wanted to follow a pattern of low interest rates as it had done during World War

II. This, of course, required price support activities since interest rates would have gone up in a free market as the demand for loanable funds increased.

The controversy between the Treasury and the Federal Reserve System developed into open conflict during the summer of 1950.[2] The controversy intensified after the Federal Reserve System had to engage in large-scale, open-market operations to keep interest rates below free-market levels as an aid in financing outstanding government debt.

President Truman appointed a committee to determine how to provide the necessary restraint on private credit expansion and at the same time, to maintain stability in the market for government securities. Before this committee could report, however, an agreement was reached between the Treasury and the Federal Reserve in early 1951. This accord was designed to check credit expansion without the use of direct controls. Government bonds were no longer purchased by the Federal Reserve to maintain a particular pattern and level of interest rates. However, the Federal Reserve continued to buy and sell some securities to maintain an orderly market.

## The 1953–1954 Recession

Business continued to advance during the first half of 1953, but by summer the rate of increase in business activity had slowed down and there was some concern that a business decline might occur. The Federal Reserve System eased credit in order to reduce the probability of a recession. In spite of this, a downturn did begin in the third quarter of 1953 and continued through the second quarter of 1954. Industrial production dropped by about 10 percent from July 1953 to May 1954, and unemployment increased to about 4 million. Gross national product decreased by only about 2 percent and personal income remained almost constant during the recession. Expenditures on construction leveled off in the second half of 1953 and the first quarter of 1954 and then increased rapidly during the remainder of the year, partly in response to lower interest rates.

The 1953–1954 downturn was largely a response to a lower level of defense expenditures, which occurred after the Korean War ended in August 1953. Reduced defense expenditures also led to some decline in business investment and to liquidation of inventories in late 1953 and 1954. Consumers also cut back moderately on durable goods expenditures, particularly for automobiles. This was partly because most consumers had late-model cars due to previous large-scale purchases. It also was due to the uncertainty of the economic outlook as unemployment increased.

This readjustment to a lower level of government purchases and the resulting decline in investment expenditures and ultimately in inventories did not result in a severe recession. There were several moderating factors. Personal income held up fairly well during the business decline partly because most sectors of the economy were not severely affected, and also because personal taxes were cut by over $3 billion. Unemployment compensation also helped cushion the decline in the personal income of the unemployed.

Economic activity increased rapidly in 1955 and personal consumption expenditures increased, especially on durable goods.[3] Automobile sales increased from about 5.5 million cars in 1954 to nearly 8 million in 1955. Residential construction increased by over $3 billion from 1954 to 1955 and declined somewhat in 1956 and 1957. Inflationary pressures began to develop during this prosperity period. To prevent serious inflation, the Federal Reserve System followed a highly restrictive monetary policy. Reserve requirements were raised, and the rediscount rate was increased on several occasions.

## The 1957–1958 Recession and Recovery

In the late summer of 1957 the economy experienced the beginning of the third postwar recession. The recession was the most severe of the three postwar readjustments that had occurred up to that time, but the period of decline was the shortest. Industrial production dropped 13 percent between August 1957 and April 1958, compared with 10 percent in the two earlier recessions. By August 1958 unemployment had increased to 7.7 percent of the civilian labor force. Gross national product declined 2.5 percent, but disposable personal income changed little due to the effect of the automatic stabilizers.

All sectors of the economy were not affected uniformly by the recession. One of the hardest hit sectors was the capital goods industry. Business expenditures on plant and equipment dropped by 16 percent. Consumer durable goods expenditures also declined, especially for automobiles.

One of the major factors leading to the decline in production and in the gross national product was the liquidation of inventories. In the third quarter of 1957, inventories were being accumulated at a rate of more than $2 billion per year. During the first quarter of 1958, inventory liquidation was at an annual rate of $9.5 billion, and in the second quarter at $8 billion.

A number of other causal factors were responsible for the 1957–1958 recession. One was the decline in capital expenditures because plant and equipment had been expanded faster than the increase in demand for goods and services. Another was the changing composition of consumer expenditures. Less money was spent on durable goods and more on nondurables and services.

Shifts in foreign trade also affected the economy during the 1957 downturn. Exports of goods and services increased in the early part of 1957 because of the crisis in Egypt and the Middle East, which closed the Suez Canal and disrupted oil exports from that region. However, once the Suez Canal was reopened in 1958, U.S. exports declined.

Economic activity reached a low point in April 1958 and then began to increase. The gains in production came in part from the ending of inventory liquidation in the last quarter of 1958 and because of some increase of inventories during the first quarter of 1959. In addition, a major force for recovery came from the consumer sector as expenditures increased on nondurable goods and services. There was also an increase in residential construction as interest rates declined and mortgage funds were made more readily available under FHA and VA programs.[4]

Higher government expenditures also helped raise business activity. Federal government expenditures increased by almost $3 billion from the third quarter of 1957 to the third quarter of 1958, and state and local government expenditures increased by almost $4 billion. By the spring of 1959, economic activity had exceeded the prerecession levels in most sectors of the economy. Unemployment remained a problem, however, since it was at 6 percent of the labor force during 1959 as compared to about 4 percent in the 1955–1957 prosperity period.

The first half of 1959 was a period of strong economic recovery that appeared to be turning into a boom. However, the economy suffered a severe setback when the longest steel strike on record began during the summer. When the steel strike ended in November 1959, there was a new surge in economic activity. Inventories were rebuilt rapidly through the first quarter of 1960, and production and gross national product reached new highs by midyear.

## The 1960–1961 Recession

The fourth postwar recession began in May of 1960. Industrial production fell during the second half of the year and into early 1961. Gross national product declined somewhat during the last quarter of 1960 and fell somewhat more in the first quarter of 1961. Unemployment, however, was more severe than in earlier postwar recessions. It had risen to unusually high levels in the 1957–1958 recession (compared to earlier postwar downturns) and continued to be a problem during the recovery period. During the 1960–1961 recession unemployment almost reached the 1958 peak even though the former downturn in production was comparatively mild. One reason for the increased unemployment was the growing size of the labor force due to a relatively high birth rate after 1939. Another cause was the accelerated pace of automation resulting from new technological advances and rising labor costs. Finally the relatively weak recovery in 1958–1960 resulted in unemployment remaining at high levels.

The 1960–1961 recession was caused by several factors. As indicated above, inventories that had been depleted by the steel strike were rebuilt rapidly in the first quarter of 1960 and then more slowly in the second quarter. This accumulation resulted in an increase in production that could not be sustained when inventory growth ceased in the third quarter. Residential construction also declined since the backlog of deferred demand had been satisfied. Moreover, mortgage money for residential financing was harder and more costly to obtain than was the case during the 1957–1958 downturn and early recovery period. Consumer buying also weakened somewhat after midyear, especially in the purchase of durable goods. Rapid increases in the volume of consumer credit outstanding in 1959 and in the first half of 1960 caused consumers subsequently to slow down purchases in order to increase their equity position.

## The Prosperity Period of the 1960s

The prosperity period that followed the mild recession of 1960–1961 was the longest in the nation's history. Some slowing in the rate of advance in economic activity occurred in late 1962; it was more pronounced in the industrial sector than the economy as a whole. There was a strong upswing in economic activity in 1965 and especially 1966 as American involvement in the Vietnam War increased greatly. Policies that were designed to reduce inflation led to a slowdown in the rate of economic growth during the first quarter of 1967, but the economy then grew rapidly from the second quarter of that year until late 1969.

Several characteristics of the early years of this prosperity period (before it was affected by the Vietnam War) are somewhat unusual. Wholesale prices remained almost completely stable from 1961 through 1964 and then began to move upward slowly in 1965 as demand accelerated. Labor cost per unit of output remained relatively constant throughout the period from 1961 through 1966. This was because wage increases generally did not exceed average gains in productivity. Moreover, major expenditures by industry on more efficient plants and equipment also helped keep labor costs stable.

The money supply was also increased gradually during most of this period. Although there was a reduction in the money supply during the early part of 1962, the supply was increased sharply in the second half of that year in response to a slowing in the rate of economic growth. From 1961–1965, the federal government realized a cash deficit that did not vary significantly in amount.

The above discussion is not meant to imply that no economic problems occurred during this era of strong economic advance. The unemployment rate did not fall below 5 percent of the labor force until late 1964, and unemployment was especially severe among teenagers throughout most of the 1960s. The Vietnam War led to additional demands for military personnel, goods, and services, but even under the stimulus of defense spending, the overall unemployment rate did not drop much below 4 percent. Many of those who were unemployed during 1965–1969 were for all practical purposes unemployable in a technologically advanced economy without an upgrading of their labor skills.

The balance of payments deficit also persisted during this period of prosperity. Efforts to increase exports were partially successful, and foreign investment by U.S. firms was reduced by a "Voluntary Foreign Credit Restraint" program. The measures taken were not sufficient, however, to eliminate the balance of payments deficit.

A new problem developed in 1966, when interest rates climbed to the highest levels since the early 1920s. The demand for funds from all sectors of the economy was strong and increasing, especially the demand for bank loans from business. To prevent serious inflation arising out of growth in demand associated with the Vietnam War, the Federal Reserve raised the discount rate in December 1965 and restricted the supply of money and credit. One result was a slowdown in residential construction during the summer of 1966. The stock market also reacted to higher interest rates and reduced profit prospects; by mid-1966 the average price of industrial common stocks had dropped some 20 percent from the peak reached in 1965.

There were signs in late 1966 that economic growth was slackening. The Federal Reserve acted to stimulate the economy by increasing the money supply at the end of the year as well as during the first half of 1967. Economic activity slowed down in the first quarter of 1967, when real GNP did not increase over the fourth quarter of 1966. There followed a very sharp recovery in economic activity in the second half of 1967 that continued until late 1969. Inflation continued at an accelerated rate during this period primarily because of a high level of private spending and the monetary and fiscal policies undertaken by the federal government during the 1966–1967 slowdown in economic activity. The federal budget for fiscal 1969 showed a slight surplus, and by mid-1969 the Federal Reserve was following a policy of severe credit restraint. Interest rates rose to higher levels than in 1966 and in some parts of the country were the highest since the Civil War.

## The 1969–1970 Recession

The economy experienced another mild recession in late 1969 that lasted throughout most of 1970. The recession was even milder than the one that occurred in 1960–1961 and was among the least severe in American history. Gross national product in current dollars continued to expand and declined only slightly in constant dollars. In fact, had it not been for a fairly lengthy auto strike in late 1970, it is possible that GNP would not have fallen at all. Industrial production declined by 6.6 percent from its 1969 peak and employment by 1.6 percent. The general price level continued to increase at a high rate during this recession period. The GNP implicit price deflator rose at an annual rate in excess of 5 percent.[5]

The recession was felt severely in the financial markets. The prices of common stocks declined somewhat more than in the earlier postwar recessions, but not as much as in the severe declines of 1929–1933 or 1937–1938. The prices of long-term debt securities were falling before the recession began as interest rates rose to unusually high levels and continued to do so during the first half of the recession period. A dramatic event was the failure of the Penn-Central Railroad to meets its financial obligations and its subsequent filing for bankruptcy.

This recession was not caused by inventory liquidation or a decline in business capital investment. In fact, business continued to accumulate inventories, and 1970 was a record year for capital outlays. The major cause was the restrictive monetary policy followed by the Federal Reserve in the second half of 1969 and into early 1970 in an effort to slow down the rate of inflation. Consumers also increased their level of saving to nearly a twenty-year high because of the uncertainties related to inflation and the continuation of the Vietnam War.

## The 1971–1973 Boom

As indicated above, the recession of 1969–1970 was unusually mild, and recovery began near the end of 1970. To slow the decrease in economic activity and to stimulate recovery, the Federal Reserve acted to make credit readily available. Because inflationary pressures were so strong, prices continued to increase even during the recession. The economy entered a period of slow recovery in 1971 under the stimulus of a rapidly increasing money supply during the first half of the year. To combat inflation, the president ordered a ninety-day price freeze in mid-August and established wage and price controls, which went into effect when the freeze ended. The goal was to cut price increases to an average 2.5 percent per year, while wages were limited to an average gain of 5.5 percent. These figures were based on the assumption that the rate of average productivity increase would be 3 percent per year. To help restrain prices, the growth rate of the money supply was cut substantially after midyear.

The economy continued to have balance of payments problems, which had persisted for several years. Because it was perceived that the dollar was overvalued in relation to major foreign currencies, the dollar was devalued in December of 1971 by 12 percent.

Recovery in economic activity accelerated in 1972, and by the end of the year real growth was increasing at a rapid rate. Consumer prices went up by only about 3.5 percent, the lowest rate of price inflation since 1967. This was due in large measure to price and wage controls. Federal Reserve monetary policy was expansive in the early part of the year, but late in 1972 money growth was slowed due to renewed inflationary pressures. Unemployment continued to be a serious problem even though employment increased as recovery continued primarily because of a rapid increase in some sectors of the labor force. Children born in the post–World War II baby boom were reaching the age of labor force entry. This meant that more teenagers were looking for jobs. Since they normally have a higher unemployment rate than older workers, overall unemployment rates rose as teenagers became a higher proportion of the total labor force. More women, who historically have had a higher unemployment rate than men, were also seeking employment.

These inflationary pressures continued and became greater in 1973, a year in which consumer prices increased some 9 percent. It appeared in early 1973 as if the year would be characterized by strong economic activity. American involvement in the Vietnam War ended early in the year, the dollar was devalued by 10 percent in February, and the persistent balance of payments problem seemed to be diminishing as America developed a surplus in its trade balance with the rest of the world. Mandatory price controls were replaced in January with more or less voluntary controls. The growth of consumer credit was slowed and the federal government had a budget surplus by the second quarter of the year.

Economic activity increased at a rapid rate and demand in many fields was in excess of supply. Price controls also led to distortions in many sectors of the economy, thus adding to shortages of some commodities. Prices rose so rapidly that a new sixty-day price freeze was put into effect in June, and at the end of the period prices were only permitted to increase by the amount that production costs rose for these items. Provisions were made for subsequent decontrol on an industry-by-industry basis.

Inflationary pressures worsened as the year progressed. This occurred for several reasons. There were poor crops in many parts of the world (including the United States), which resulted in higher prices of food products. Large amounts of wheat were sold to Russia and China, leading to rapid increases in grain prices. In October another Arab-Israeli War took place, but it was of short duration. The Arabs, in order to put pressure on the United States and other countries to support their interests, placed an embargo on oil shipments to Western countries and raised oil prices. The embargo was lifted after a period but the prices of petroleum products rose to several times their prewar levels.

The demand for credit remained high. Monetary policy caused the supply of credit to be restricted and as a result, interest rates reached unprecedentedly high levels. The boom in 1973 was so strong that it probably would not have lasted even if the Federal Reserve had not acted to restrict the growth of credit.

## The 1973–1975 Recession

The recession, which began late in 1973, was the longest and most severe of the post–World War II business declines. The recession began in November 1973 and lasted through March 1975, a period of 16 months. Real GNP in terms of 1972 prices declined by 6.6 percent. This was more than twice the decline that occurred in the recession of 1957–1958, the second most severe of the postwar business slumps. From late 1973 until May 1975, industrial production dropped almost 15 percent.

Construction also declined significantly. Total construction contracts in early 1975 were 25 percent below the average level in 1973. Housing experienced an even more dramatic decline from a level of 2.4 million starts in 1973 to a low of 880,000 on an annual basis at the end of 1974.[6]

Changes in inventories generally lag behind movements in GNP, but the lag was unusual in this recession. Inventories increased in each quarter of 1974, although for different reasons. In the first two quarters, inventories rose as producers attempted to build stocks that had previously been in short supply. During the last two quarters, inventories grew because sales declined and stocks had become excessive in relation to sales. This was particularly the case in the last quarter of 1974. There was a severe liquidation of inventories in the first two quarters of 1975, and the liquidation continued at a slower pace during the remainder of the year.

Employment dropped from a record 79.9 million in October 1974 to 76.6 million in February 1975. Three-fourths of the reduction was in manufacturing. The unemployment rate rose to a postwar high of 9.2 percent in the spring of 1975.[7] Prices rose rapidly during the recession instead of declining or rising more slowly, as generally occurred in earlier cycles. The GNP deflator rose almost 10 percent in 1974 compared with less than 6 percent in 1973. Consumer prices also increased rapidly, rising at an 11 percent rate in 1974.[8]

Interest rates also rose to unprecedented levels in 1974. Near the end of April, the Federal Reserve raised the discount rate to 8 percent and late in June and early in July the federal funds rate averaged a record 13.5 percent. On July 3, major banks raised their prime rates to a record 12 percent. The combination of high interest rates and poor business conditions led to a major decline in stock prices. Early in December the Dow Jones Industrial Average closed at 578, the lowest level since October 1963, and well below the high for the year of 892 reached in mid-March.[9]

Several events in the financial sector contributed to the overall severity of the recession. In April 1974, Consolidated Edison omitted a dividend for the first time in its history; and in May, the Franklin National Bank did not pay a dividend due to foreign exchange losses. In early October the Comptroller of the Currency declared the Franklin National Bank insolvent. New York City also had continuing problems in meeting payments on debts, but partly because of federal and state assistance was able to keep from being declared in default.[10]

The 1973–1975 recession was experienced throughout the industrialized world. The growth of output in the first half of 1973 in France, West Germany, Italy, the United Kingdom, Japan, and Canada was at an exceptionally high rate. This was followed by an equally sharp decline in output in nearly all industrialized countries and a general recession.[11] In some nations the recession was the most severe since World War II, just as it was in the United States.

However, the recession of 1973–1975 also differed from earlier postwar declines in that it consisted of two distinct phases. The first phase was a response to constraints on aggregate supply. The second phase, which began in the early fall of 1974, also reflected a major reduction in demand for goods and services.

Total spending for goods and services rose substantially during the first three quarters of the recession. Monetary growth continued to be rapid during the first two quarters of the recession, whereas business declines are frequently characterized by slow growth of the money supply. As indicated above, the chief cause of the economic downturn during this period came from limitations of aggregate supply. The ability of the nation to produce was reduced by increased energy costs, the expenses associated with environmental and safety programs, unfavorable weather and insect infestations leading to lowered agricultural production, and the unbalancing effects on production of price controls. The result was a decline in the quantity of goods available for consumption and an increase in prices. The second phase of the recession was characterized by the more typical lack of demand. Total spending declined sharply in the last quarter of 1974 and the first quarter of 1975.

## Causes of the 1973–1975 Recession

Like all severe recessions, the recession of 1973–1975 had both immediate and longer-run causal factors. The major proximate cause of the downturn was severe inflation. This was partly attributable to the relatively easy monetary and fiscal policy in the years preceding 1973. This was generally true not only in the United States, but in all major industrialized countries. There were also several additional factors contributing to worldwide inflation. Farm prices went up rapidly in 1973 due to poor crops in many parts of the world. Oil prices also rose dramatically due to the actions of Organization of Petroleum Exporting Countries (OPEC). There was an increase in raw material prices generally as worldwide demand rose more rapidly than supply. Inflation not only had an effect on interest rates and stock prices, but also on consumption patterns. Increased prices for oil products and food left consumers with less money for other items. Wage rates rose less rapidly than consumer prices, resulting in a decline in real wages. In addition, higher money wages pushed consumers into higher tax brackets thus lowering after-tax real income. (This phenomenon is known as "bracket creep.")

As mentioned above, excessive inventory buildup helped bring about the recession. Goods became so scarce during the 1972–1973 boom that many businesses failed to see the portending economic decline and continued to build stocks. When inventories had to be liquidated, demand was further reduced and the recession intensified.

A wave of speculation had occurred in the real estate industry during 1972–73. Real estate investment trusts supplied high-risk construction loans for condominiums, recreational housing, and shopping centers and malls. This resulted in considerable over-building in certain regions. Thus, by 1972 the vacancy rate for office buildings reached 13 percent and many projects were in serious financial trouble.[12]

Fiscal policy was not used to stop the speculative excesses but in fact became more expansive. Taxes were reduced in 1964, 1965, 1969, and 1971, and spending was increased for social programs and the war in Vietnam. Corporations allowed their equity positions to deteriorate and their overall liquidity to decline. Large banks relied more heavily on volatile short-term funds to finance their lending activities and some state and local governments followed unsafe financial practices, including excessive short-term borrowing. The need to correct such excesses served to intensify the 1973–1975 recession.

## Recovery from the 1973–1975 Recession

Recovery from the recession began in the fourth quarter of 1975. To stimulate recovery, monetary policy became much more expansive early in 1975. Fiscal policy became somewhat stimulative late in 1974 and quite expansionary in 1975 because of an increase in expenditures and a sizable tax cut. The latter was particularly beneficial to lower income individuals. Interest rates declined from the high levels of 1973 and 1974 and thereby made investment easier to finance. Inflation also slowed as the recession deepened.

Consumers helped the recovery by increasing spending on nondurable goods. As excessive inventories were finally drawn down, increased production was necessary to meet current demand. Recovery was also helped by the trade surplus, which hit a record level in 1975 as imports were reduced and exports expanded.

Economic activity continued to expand in 1976 and into 1977 as the recovery moved forward. Despite the remaining economic problems, such as excessive inflation and high unemployment, it appeared that the economy was well on the way to a healthy and sustained recovery in 1977.

## The Recession of 1980

On June 3, 1980, the National Bureau of Economic Research's Committee on Business Cycle Dating indicated that the recession of 1980 had begun in January 1980. Following a long period of very little economic growth in 1979, most of the important economic indicators of macroeconomic activity declined early in 1980. The movements formed a sufficiently consistent pattern to denote a transition from a phase of slow growth to one of a cyclical decline. Similar slowdown-and-recession sequences have been observed during many previous business cycles.

Although housing construction and manufacturing had weakened the year before the recession began, services and business fixed investment held up relatively well during 1979. The personal saving rate fell to unusually low levels in this period of widely anticipated inflation and low real interest rates, a situation that helped to boost the economy temporarily despite the slow erosion of real after-tax income within a large part of the private sector. The decline in economic activity accelerated greatly in the spring quarter. Real GNP fell at a record annual rate of 9.9 percent during the second quarter of 1980.[13]

In mid-March, credit restraints of unprecedented severity in peacetime were suddenly imposed by the Federal Reserve. The reaction to this unanticipated monetary policy turned out to be very strong. For example, total private borrowing fell 51 percent in the second quarter of 1980.[14] At the same time, growth rates of monetary aggregates fell sharply, with some measures of the money supply actually experiencing an absolute decline. Partly as a result, interest rates rose rapidly to peaks of 14–20 percent in March and April, and then fell abruptly to 7–12 percent in June and July.

The phase of rapid contraction was of short duration. The Federal Reserve acted in May of 1980 to soften the credit controls and eliminated them completely on July 3. Private borrowing increased strongly during the third quarter of 1980. Reduced rates of increase in consumer prices and declines in interest rates helped improve consumer expectations and buying attitudes. Real retail sales and housing starts began to increase. The decline in the National Bureau of Economic Research coincident index of economic activity came to a halt in June–August, and the decline in real GNP was arrested during the third quarter of 1980. These events had been signaled by the leading index of economic indicators, which reached its lowest point in May.

The initial rise in the latter index was as large as it usually is early in a business recovery—over 12 percent between May and November 1980. Correspondingly, activity picked up strongly in many areas of the economy, although some, notably the automobile industry, remained depressed. Thus, industrial production gained 6.4 percent in July–November (over 20 percent on an annual basis).[15]

Monetary growth accelerated greatly in the summer and fall of 1980. Fears that the new surge of money and credit creation would result in greater inflationary pressures, and that the Federal Reserve would once again precipitate a drastic retrenchment, helped bring about a second round of sharp interest rises within one year. Thus, the prime rate rose above 20 percent (its previous high of late April) in the second half of December 1980. Given actual inflation rates, the burden in real terms of these money costs was high and brought widespread concern that the recovery would be relatively brief.

Although the 1980 recession was short (about six months in length), the drop in real GNP was larger than the declines in three of the six previous post–World War II recessions. The comparisons for industrial production indicate the contraction was of average severity. Only in terms of the changes in employment and unemployment can the 1980 recession be considered the mildest of the seven episodes since 1948. The trend toward milder declines in employment has been occurring for many years, largely because of the growth in employment in the service industries, which as a rule are more recession-insulated than the goods-producing industries.

Real GNP increased at a 2.4 percent annual rate in the third quarter and at a 4.0 percent annual rate in the fourth quarter of 1980. The first of these figures falls short of, but the second exceeds, the long-term growth rate of U.S. aggregate output.

## The 1981–1982 Recession

The recovery that began in August of 1980 was one of the shortest on record, lasting only eleven months. Because it was a relatively weak recovery, unemployment barely declined from the recession peak. Reaching a level of 7.8 percent in July 1980, it had fallen only to 7.4 percent by July of 1981.

Inflation remained at double-digit levels in 1980 and early 1981. Partly because of this high level of inflation, monetary policy remained very tight. The combination of restrictive monetary policy and high inflation pushed interest rates to record levels in nominal terms. By the spring of 1981, the prime interest rate was nearly 20 percent, compared to slightly more than 11 percent in mid-1980.[16]

The high interest rates were responsible for a sharp decline in purchases of new homes and automobiles. Consumer spending on such items as furniture and household equipment and state and local government construction are also responsive to interest rates. Declines in consumer spending and housing construction were major causes of the sixteen-month recession that began in July 1981 and resulted in an increase in unemployment to the highest levels since 1941.

Inventory liquidation was large in the fourth quarter of 1981 and the first quarter of 1982. This contributed substantially to the approximately 5 percent decline in GNP during those two quarters. Declines in auto production accounted for about one-third of the GNP decline from July 1981 to March 1982.[17] By the fall of 1982, the prime rate had fallen to just over 13 percent, the result of easier monetary policy, somewhat lower inflation, and a decline in the demand for loanable funds.

By November 1982, 12 million persons were unemployed. This level was 50 percent more than that in the third quarter of 1981 and double that in the second quarter of 1979, the low prior to the 1980 recession. As a percentage of the civilian labor force, unemployed persons were at a postwar high of 10.8 percent in November, up from 7.4 percent in the third quarter of 1981 and from 5.7 percent in the second quarter of 1979.[18]

Real GNP declined 2 percent in the fourth quarter of 1982. Although personal consumption expenditures were up sharply, especially in the durable goods sector, where lower interest rates stimulated demand, nonresidential fixed investment declined further in part due to poor profits and low rates of capacity utilization. Imports declined but exports declined even more, reflecting the dollar's appreciation and the worldwide recession. Business inventories, which increased $7 billion in the third quarter of 1982, fell by $14 billion in the fourth quarter of 1982.[19]

The Economic Recovery Tax Act (ERTA) of 1981 was passed shortly before Congress adjourned and was signed in mid-August. The major features of the act were the following:[20]

1. a 25 percent across-the-board reduction in individual income taxes*
   over 33 months—5 percent on October 1, 1981 and 10 percent on
   July 1, 1982 and July 1, 1983

---

*Since 1985, income tax brackets, the zero bracket amount, and the personal exemption have been adjusted for inflation as a result of ERTA.

## Table 4–1
### Selected Measures of Duration, Depth, and Diffusion of Business Cycle Contractions, 1948–1982

| | Nov. 1948–Oct. 1949 (1) | July 1953–May 1954 (2) | Aug. 1957–Apr. 1958 (3) | Apr. 1960–Feb. 1961 (4) | Dec. 1969–Nov. 1970 (5) | Nov. 1973–Mar. 1975 (6) | Jan. 1980–July 1980 (7) | July 1981–Nov. 1982 (8) |
|---|---|---|---|---|---|---|---|---|
| *Duration*[a] | | | | | | | | |
| Business cycle | 11 | 12 | 8 | 10 | 11 | 16 | 6 | 16 |
| GNP, constant dollars | 6 | 12 | 6 | 10 | 15 | 15 | 3 | 16 |
| Coincident index | 12 | 15 | 14 | 13 | 13 | 16 | 6 | 16 |
| Industrial production | 15 | 9 | 13 | 13 | 13 | 9 | 6 | 16 |
| Nonfarm employment | 13 | 16 | 14 | 10 | 8 | 6 | 5 | 17 |
| *Depth (%)*[b] | | | | | | | | |
| GNP, constant dollars | -1.4 | -3.3 | -3.2 | -1.2 | -1.1 | -5.7 | -2.6 | -3.0 |
| Coincident index | -10.8 | -9.2 | -12.4 | -6.8 | -6.3 | -13.9 | -7.0 | -11.0 |
| Industrial production | -10.1 | -9.4 | -13.5 | -8.6 | -6.8 | -15.3 | -8.5 | -12.5 |
| Nonfarm employment | -5.2 | -3.4 | -4.3 | -2.2 | -1.6 | -3.7 | -1.4 | -1.6 |

*Unemployment rate*

| | | | | | | | |
|---|---|---|---|---|---|---|---|
| Maximum | 7.9 | 6.1 | 7.5 | 7.1 | 6.1 | 9.1 | 7.6 | 10.8 |
| Increase | +4.5 | +3.6 | +3.8 | +2.3 | +2.7 | +4.2 | +2.0 | +3.4 |

Sources: U.S. Department of Commerce, U.S. Department of Labor, Board of Governors of the Federal Reserve System, National Bureau of Economic Research.

aFrom peak (first date) to trough (second date).

bPercentage change from the peak month or quarter in the series to the trough month or quarter over the intervals shown above. For the unemployment rate, the maximum figure is the highest for any month associated with the contraction, and the increases are from the lowest month to the highest, in percentage points.

2. an accelerated cost recovery system that provides substantially faster depreciation write-offs for business

3. a substantial reduction in estate and gift taxes

Personal tax and nontax receipts were reduced $3.9 billion in 1981 and $41.2 billion in 1982. Most of the reduction was in income tax withholding.

The tax cut plus increased government purchases of goods and services and transfer payments led to substantial increases in disposable income. This factor, together with lower interest rates, led the economy out of recession, and 1983 and 1984 witnessed a vigorous recovery.

Although some slowdown in nominal GNP growth and in inflation in 1982 was a predictable effect of tighter monetary policies, the very sharp decline actually experienced did not reflect a decrease in the growth of the monetary aggregates. Rather the exceptional severity of the slowdown in nominal GNP growth can be traced to a combination of factors that led to an unusually sharp decline in the velocity of money, that is, in the ratio of GNP to the money stock. (See chapter 6 for further discussion of this point.)

If this velocity shift had not occurred, the rise in nominal GNP in 1982 would have been 10 and 12 percent. While it is uncertain how this hypothetical change would have been distributed between real activity and inflation, it is likely that real GNP would have increased enough to have ended the recession sometime before the final quarter of 1982.[21]

Table 4–1 compares selected economic statistics for the eight postwar recessions. The mildest recession was the 1969–1970 recession, while the 1973–1975 decline was the most severe in the postwar period. Employment declined more in the 1948–1949 recession than during any subsequent downturns even though, based on other criteria, the 1948–1949 recession was not especially severe. In the late 1940s, however, a larger fraction of the labor force was employed in cyclically sensitive industries than in later years.

From 1982–1985 employment increased more than 9 million. Real business investment has sustained the largest increase of any comparable period in the postwar era. Interest rates declined 5 percentage points from their peaks in 1981 and home mortgage rates were down by 7 percentage points.[22] Inflation was about one-third of the level reached in the early 1980s.

## Summary

There have been eight business recessions since the end of World War II, lasting an average of eleven months. For the most part they have been mild to moderate in depth; only the 1973–1975 recession could be characterized as severe.

Unemployment has been highest when the preceding recovery has been of short duration. Thus, in early 1961 unemployment was nearly at a postwar high because of the weak recovery from the recession of 1957–1958. Moreover, the 1981–1982 recession resulted in record postwar unemployment of 12 million because the preceding recovery lasted only a year, and the 1981–1982 recession was 16 months in length. In fact GNP at the end of 1982 was less than GNP in 1979.

As a generalization, the postwar recessions can be characterized as "inventory" recessions; that is, the business cycle contractions have been the result of excessive inventory accumulation and subsequent liquidation. Personal income and consumption spending have been stabilizing factors that have prevented many of the postwar recessions from becoming more severe.

A tight monetary policy in response to severe inflationary pressure has been a major contributing factor with regard to the last three recessions. High interest rates have been a major causal factor in the decline in durable goods purchases (especially automobiles) and residential and nonresidential construction.

Tax cuts, such as those that occurred in the 1953–1954 and 1981–1982 recessions helped to moderate those contractions. In addition, the automatic stabilizers and accompanying federal budget deficits helped to move the economy toward the recovery phase of the cycle.

# Notes

1. U.S. Department of Commerce, *Economic Report of the President, 1983* (Washington, D.C.: U.S. Government Printing Office, 1983), pp. 165 and 188.

2. Carl Dauten and Lloyd Valentine, *Business Cycles and Forecasting*, 5th ed. (Dallas, Tex.: South-Western Publishing Co., 1978), p. 294.

3. U.S. Department of Commerce, op.cit., p. 171.

4. Dauten and Valentine, op.cit., pp. 296–97.

5. Solomon Fabricant, *Recent Economic Changes and the Agenda of Business-Cycle Research* (New York: National Bureau of Economic Research, Inc., 1971), p. 27.

6. *Federal Reserve Bulletin*, February 1976, p. A-50.

7. Ibid., p. A-52.

8. Ibid., pp. A-53–A-55.

9. Federal Reserve Bank of Chicago, *Business Conditions*, January 1975, pp. 16–17.

10. Ibid.

11. "Inflation and Stagnation in Major Foreign Industrial Countries," *Federal Reserve Bulletin*, October 1974, pp. 683–98.

12. Arthur Burns, "Causes of the 1973–1975 Recession," *Federal Reserve Bulletin*, May 1975, pp. 273–79.

13. Victor Zarnowitz and Geoffrey Moore, "The Timing and Severity of the 1980 Recession," in *Business Cycles, Inflation and Forecasting*, 2d ed., Geoffrey Moore, National Bureau of Economic Research, Studies in Business Cycles, no. 24 (Cambridge, Mass.: Ballinger Publishing Co., 1983), p. 12.

14. Ibid., p. 14.

15. Ibid., pp. 14 and 16.

16. U.S. Department of Commerce, "The Business Situation," *Survey of Current Business*, June 1981, p. 3.

17. U.S. Department of Commerce, "The Business Situation," *Survey of Current Business*, May 1982, p. 1.

18. U.S. Department of Commerce, "The Business Situation " *Survey of Current Business*, December 1982, p. 6.

19. U.S. Department of Commerce, "The Business Situation," *Survey of Current Business*, January 1983, p. 1.

20. U.S. Department of Commerce, "The Business Situation," *Survey of Current Business*, August 1981, p. 5.

21. U.S. Department of Commerce, op.cit., p. 21.

22. U.S. Department of Commerce, *Economic Report of the President, 1986* (Washington, D.C.: U.S. Government Printing Office, 1986), p. 23.

# 5
# Some Effects of Business Cycles

I t is common to divide the sources of growth in potential output into two broad areas: growth in inputs (capital, labor, land) and improvements in technology or efficiency. Using statistical techniques, one can estimate the quantitative contribution of each of these growth factors.

For example, consider the 1948–1981 period. During this time real potential output is estimated to have grown at 3.3 percent per annum. Growth in labor inputs accounted for about 20 percent of the gain in total output, 15 percent was attributed to a larger capital stock, and 33 percent of the output increase was due to improved knowledge and technology. The remaining 32 percent was accounted for by miscellaneous sources.[1]

Estimates of the gain in potential output indicate that the growth path is subject to some change. Thus, potential output grew at 3.82 percent per year from 1948 to 1973, but at only 2.66 percent per year from 1973 to 1982.[2] It is unusual to observe such rapid changes in the growth of the economy's potential output. The cyclical movement of economic activity causes the gap between potential and actual GNP to become larger or to diminish. Business cycles also affect employment and unemployment and, indirectly, health status.

## Okun's Law

An increase in unemployment is a universal occurrence in recessions. As orders and output fall, workers are laid off. Wage rigidity prevents workers from readily finding new jobs at lower wage rates. Thus, during the contraction phase of the business cycle, the rate of unemployment increases. Table 5–1 indicates the close relationship between output changes and unemployment. This relationship was first discovered by the late Arthur Okun and is consequently called Okun's Law.

Okun's Law states that for every 2 percent that GNP declines relative to potential GNP, the unemployment rate rises 1 percentage point. Thus, if

Table 5–1
**Relationships Between Potential Output and the Unemployment Rate, 1955–1982**

| Year | Unemployment Rate | Output Gap[a] |
|------|------|------|
| 1955 | 4.3 | −0.7 |
| 1958 | 6.6 | +6.3 |
| 1960 | 5.4 | +3.9 |
| 1961 | 6.5 | +4.9 |
| 1962 | 5.4 | +2.2 |
| 1965 | 4.4 | −1.4 |
| 1970 | 4.8 | +4.3 |
| 1971 | 5.8 | +4.4 |
| 1973 | 4.8 | +3.0 |
| 1975 | 8.3 | +8.0 |
| 1977 | 6.9 | +5.1 |
| 1979 | 5.8 | +5.0 |
| 1980 | 7.0 | +8.0 |
| 1981 | 7.5 | +7.3 |
| 1982 | 9.5 | +10.7 |

Sources: Unemployment data from U.S. Department of Commerce, *Economic Report of the President*, 1987 (Washington D.C.: U.S. Government Printing Office, 1987), p. 285. Output gap calculated from Edward Dennison, *Trends in American Economic Growth, 1929–1982*, (Washington D.C.: The Brookings Institution, 1985), p. 115.

[a]The output gap is measured as the percentage deviation of actual GNP from potential GNP.

GNP begins at 100 percent of its potential and falls to 98 percent of potential GNP, the unemployment rate would rise, for example, from 4 to 5 percent.

Assuming that potential GNP is growing at 3 percent annually—which is the approximate rate for the 1975–1985 decade, to keep the unemployment rate constant requires that real GNP also grow at 3 percent each year. In other words, production must keep increasing just to keep the unemployment rate constant.

During the period from 1979 to 1982, actual output remained unchanged but potential GNP grew at 3 percent per annum. Thus, from 1979 to 1982 potential GNP increased by over 9 percent. Under the circumstances what should have happened to the unemployment rate? According to Okun's Law each 2 percent gap between actual and potential output adds 1 percentage point to the unemployment rate. A 9 percent gap in GNP should have led to a rise in the unemployment rate of 4.5 percentage points. Beginning with an unemployment rate of 5.8 percent in 1979, Okun's Law would predict a 10.3 percent unemployment rate in 1982. The official statistics show the actual unemployment rate for 1982 was 9.7 percent.[3] In this case, the discrepancy between actual and predicted unemployment was small.

## The Unemployed in Prosperity and Recession

According to Okun's Law, during periods when unemployment is high, actual GNP is well below its potential level. Thus, above average unemployment is associated with high levels of lost output. How much forgone output is associated with high unemployment? Table 5–2 indicates how far output has fallen below potential GNP during three periods of high unemployment over the last fifty years. While the major loss occurred during the Great Depression, during the slow growth period of the 1970s and 1980s the economy has experienced more than a trillion dollars in lost output.

Moreover, recessions can have harmful effects on productivity long after they have officially ended. Investments in both physical and human resources that could add to our productivity in the future are undertaken less frequently during periods of unemployment and idle capacity. Other productivity losses occur because the skills of some jobless workers become obsolete.

In order to determine the impact of business conditions on the labor market, it is useful to compare jobless rates (for various groups) when unemployment is low (as in 1973) with unemployment rates during recession (1982).

During a period of prosperity, a large proportion of unemployment is

**Table 5–2**
**Economic Loss During Periods of High Unemployment**

| Period | Average Unemployment Rate (percent) | Lost Output Billions (1982 $) | As Percent of Average Annual GNP during the Period |
|---|---|---|---|
| 1930–1939 | 18.2 | $1981 | 325 |
| 1954–1960 | 5.2 | 63 | 4 |
| 1975–1984 | 7.6 | 1228 | 39 |

Source: Calculated from data contained in Robert Gordon, *Macroeconomics*, 4th ed. (Boston: Little Brown & Co., 1987), appendix A, table A-1, pp. 582–83.

termed *frictional*. This unemployment category includes unemployed new entrants to the labor force and the seasonally unemployed, as well as those individuals who voluntarily quit one job and are currently unemployed because they have not been able to find another position.[4] Much frictional unemployment is thus independent of the general business cycle; but certainly not all, since voluntary resignation rates as well as labor force participation rates of secondary earners are positively related to overall economic activity.

Cyclical unemployment reflects changes in the number of jobless workers as a result of fluctuations in overall economic activity. During a period of severe recession or depression, most unemployment is of a cyclical nature as opposed to the situation during prosperity, when, as indicated above, the majority of job seekers can be classified as frictionally unemployed. The burden of cyclical unemployment is not evenly distributed. Some industries and occupations suffer major declines in employment, while others are essentially insulated from variations in overall economic activity. Employment in manufacturing, especially durable goods manufacturing, is quite sensitive to business fluctuations. Employment in the service industries, however, has shown a persistent upward trend for many years that is relatively unaffected by changes in economic conditions. Because our economy has gradually shifted from goods producing to services, shifts in economic activity have a smaller effect on overall employment levels than previously.

Several comparative aspects of the labor market can be noted from an examination of table 5–3, which presents unemployment data for both of the above periods. First note that recession tends to affect all demographic groups in approximately the same relative degree. That is, when the unemployment rate doubles (as was roughly the case from 1973 to 1982), the unemployment rate within each group increases about 100 percent. This means that the unemployment rate in groups with high rates (such as Blacks) goes up much more in absolute terms than it does among those with low unemployment rates (such as whites). However, no segment of society is completely insulated from a major economic downturn.

Nonwhites tend to experience unemployment rates twice those of whites. However, relative unemployment rates of males and females have reversed themselves over the last decade. Women have historically had higher unemployment rates than men, but this was not the case in 1982. Finally, the proportion of teenage unemployment to the total is much greater in boom than in recession. For example, in 1973, teenagers were more than one-quarter of all unemployed workers. In deep recession (1982) they were less than one-fifth.

Table 5–3
Selected Unemployment Rates, 1973 and 1982

| Labor Market Group | Unemployment Rate of Different Groups (percent of labor force) | | Unemployed in Group (percent of total unemployment) | |
|---|---|---|---|---|
| | Boom (1973) | Recession (1982) | Boom (1973) | Recession (1982) |
| *By age:* | | | | |
| 16–19 years | 14.5 | 23.2 | 18.5 | 18.5 |
| 20 years and older | 3.8 | 8.6 | 71.5 | 81.5 |
| *By race:* | | | | |
| White | 4.3 | 8.6 | 79.2 | 77.2 |
| Black and other | 8.9 | 17.3 | 20.8 | 22.8 |
| *By sex (adults only):* | | | | |
| Male | 3.3 | 8.8 | 51.8 | 58.5 |
| Female | 4.8 | 8.3 | 48.2 | 41.5 |
| All workers | 4.9 | 9.7 | 100.0 | 100.0 |

Source: U.S. Department of Commerce, *Economic Report of the President, 1987* (Washington, D.C.: U.S. Government Printing Office, 1987), pp. 280, 282, and 284.

## Duration of Unemployment

Economic fluctuations also affect the duration of unemployment. Long-term unemployment is of major social concern; short-term unemployment, which often reflects the movement of people between jobs, is of less economic and social importance.

Table 5–4 indicates the duration of unemployment in boom and recession, again using 1973 and 1982 data. A very large fraction of unemployment is of very short duration. Thus, in the boom year of 1973, less than one-fifth of unemployment lasted more than fourteen weeks. In recessions, however, it takes considerably longer to find jobs, and long-term unemployment becomes a serious economic problem. The number of workers out of a job for more than six months rose from 340,000 in 1973 to 2,600,000 at the end of 1982. In Europe, with lower geographical and social mobility and greater labor market rigidity, long-term unemployment in the early 1980s reached 50 percent of total unemployed. Long-term unemployment poses a particular problem because the resources that families have available—their savings and unemployment insurance—are usually exhausted after several months.

Table 5–4
The Duration of Unemployment

| Length of | Percent of Unemployed Workers | |
| Unemployment (weeks) | 1973 | 1982 |
|---|---|---|
| 0–14 | 52 | 37 |
| 5–14 | 29 | 32 |
| 15–26 | 10 | 15 |
| More than 26 | 9 | 16 |
| Total | 100 | 100 |

Source: U.S. Department of Commerce, *Economic Report of the President, 1987* (Washington, D.C.: U.S. Government Printing Office, 1987), p. 283.

## Causes of Joblessness

The reasons for unemployment vary considerably from boom to recession (see table 5–5). In both situations less than 1 percent of the labor force are unemployed because they left their jobs, and another 2 to 3 percent are new entrants into the labor force (perhaps because they just graduated from high school or college) or reentrants (people who had earlier left the labor force and are back looking for jobs). The major change from boom to recession is found in the fraction of job losers. From 1973 to 1982 the fraction of the labor force unemployed because they lost their jobs tripled. This source increases greatly in recession for two reasons: first the number of people who lose their jobs increases, and then (as indicated in table 5–4) it takes longer to find a new job. Moreover, during recession the breadwinner or primary earner may become unemployed. In order to prevent a major decline in living standards, other family members (secondary earners) may enter or reenter the labor force (see table 5–5).

Table 5–5
Distribution of Unemployment by Cause
(percent)

| | 1973 | 1982 |
|---|---|---|
| Job loser | 1.9 | 5.7 |
| Reentrant | 1.5 | 2.2 |
| New entrant | 0.7 | 1.1 |
| Job leaver | 0.7 | 0.8 |

Source: U.S. Department of Commerce, *Economic Report of the President, 1987* (Washington, D.C.: U.S. Government Printing Office, 1987), p. 283.

## The Impact of the 1981–1982 Recession on Unemployment

By November 1982, the rate for men was 10.1 percent, up 4.1 percentage points from the third quarter of 1981. This increase is larger than that recorded in all postwar recessions except 1949. For women, the rate was 9.1 percent, up 2.4 points, which is about the average increase for a recession. The unemployment rate for men increases more than that for women in most recessions, but it is unusual for the rate for men to increase so much that it exceeds the rate for women.

Blue collar workers experienced the sharpest increase in their unemployment rate from a level that was already the highest of the four major occupational groups. The blue collar rate was up 6.8 percentage points (from July 1981 to November 1982) to 16.5 percent in November 1982. Over the same time period, the rate for white collar workers increased the least of any major occupational group—up only 1.6 points to 5.6 percent.[5]

The sharp increase in the unemployment rates for men and for blue collar workers can be traced to the industries most affected by the weakness in economic activity. Among nonagricultural private wage and salary workers, the highest November 1982 unemployment rates, as well as the sharpest increases from 1981 lows, were for construction workers (21.9 percent in November 1982), miners (18.0 percent), and durable goods manufacturing employees (17.1 percent). In construction the increase was 6.0 percentage points. For mining and durable goods manufacturing, the increases were 12.1 and 10.0 points, respectively. These three are among the goods producing industries—the blue collar industries—where the labor force is predominantly made up of men.[6]

## The Impact of Unemployment on Health Status

Aside from the direct economic impact of joblessness, there is evidence that unemployment leads to a deterioration of both mental and physical health. Thus, research indicates that relatively high unemployment rates are associated with increased levels of heart disease, infant and maternal mortality, mental illness, and suicide. One researcher, Dr. M. Harvey Brenner, estimates that a 1-percentage point rise in the unemployment rate sustained over a period of six years would lead to 37,000 cases of premature mortality.[7] Table 5–6 shows an index of the stress caused by different "life events" ranging from death of family and friends to changing working conditions. These and other studies indicate that involuntary joblessness is a highly traumatic event for many people.

Since 1980, the United States has experienced two recessions and the

Table 5–6
Stress Associated with Joblessness and Other Events

| Life Event | Level of Stress Associated with Event |
|---|---|
| Death of spouse | 100 |
| Went to jail | 66 |
| Fired from job | 49 |
| Close friend died | 47 |
| Laid off from job | 40 |
| Failed school | 37 |
| Child left home | 29 |
| Major change in working conditions | 20 |

Source: T. H. Holmes, "The Social Readjustment Rating Scale," *Journal of Psychosomatic Research* 11 (1967) pp. 213–18; B. S. Dohrenwenrd, L. Krasnoff, A. R. Askenasy, and B. P. Dohrenwend, "The Psychiatric Epidemiology Research Interview Life Events Scale," in *Handbook of Stress*, ed. L. Goldberger and S. Breznitz (New York: Free Press, 1982), pp. 332–63.

highest levels of unemployment since the 1930s. The national unemployment rate exceeded 10 percent for ten months in 1982 and 1983. At the worst point of the 1981–1982 recession nearly 12 million people, or 10.7 percent of the work force, were unemployed. In two years unemployment rose by more than 40 percent and directly affected at least one-fourth of all persons in the work force. Among families with one or more members in the labor force, 29 percent had at least one number unemployed in 1981 and 33 percent had someone unemployed during 1982.

Using data from 1950 to 1980, Brenner examined the relationship between economic changes and nine indicators of social stress: total mortality rates, cardiovascular-renal disease mortality, cirrhosis of the liver mortality, mental hospital admissions, suicide rates, homicide rates, state prison admissions, total arrest rates, and the incidence of major crimes reported to the police. The principal economic measures are per capita income (adjusted for inflation), unemployment rates, labor force participation rates, and business failure rates.

The effects of the 14 percent increase in unemployment prior to the most severe portion of the 1973–1975 recession, summarized in table 5–7, included a 6 percent increase in admissions to state mental hospitals and a 6 percent increase in total arrests. Additional increases in social pathology

**Table 5–7**
**Impact of a 14.3 Percent Rise in Unemployment During 1973–1974**

| Pathological Indicator | Change Related to 14.3 Percent Rise in Unemployment (percent) | Increase in Incidence of Pathology |
|---|---|---|
| Total mortality | 2.3 | 45,936 |
| Cardiovascular mortality | 2.8 | 28,510 |
| Cirrhosis mortality | 1.4 | 430 |
| Suicide | 1.0 | 270 |
| Population in mental hospitals | 6.0 | 8,416 |
| Total arrests | 6.0 | 577,577 |
| Arrests for fraud and embezzlement | 4.8 | 11,552 |
| Assaults reported to police | 1.1 | 7,035 |
| Homicide[a] | 1.71 | 403 |

Source: M. Harvey Brenner, *Estimating the Effects of Economic Change on National Health and Social Well-Being*, Joint Economic Committee, Congress of the United States (Washington, D.C.: U.S. Government Printing Office, 1984), p. v.

[a]Increases in the homicide rate were found to be related to rising unemployment among males 16–24, expressed as a proportion of the total unemployment rate.

were associated with the 3 percent drop in real per capita income and the sharp rise in business failures that also occurred during this period.

With three exceptions, these figures reflect the cumulative changes in pathology rates over a six-year period. Because chronic diseases take longer to develop and detect, the changes in cardiovascular mortality, cirrhosis mortality, and total mortality were estimated to occur within sixteen years. However, the figures should be viewed as minimum estimates, since only a subset of possible problems is examined. Moreover, the measures of pathology do not capture some of the less extreme consequences—like nonfatal illness and crises that do not result in incarceration—that may have been influenced by economic factors.

Naturally, since many other variables contribute to social pathology, the rates of change associated with the economic measures appear small. The costs, in both human and dollar terms, are substantial, however. For example, over 45,000 deaths can be attributed to the rise in unemployment that occurred at the onset of the 1974-1975 recession. Moreover, the drop in real per capita income at that time brought about 60,000 deaths. The increased unemployment at this time was also linked with 27 additional suicides, 8,416 additional admissions to mental hospitals, and 577,577 additional arrests.

In interpreting these findings, it must be emphasized that Brenner's research deals only with aggregate relationships. Thus, it does not provide direct information about the behavior of individuals. As a result, someone who loses a job does not necessarily have a greater likelihood of committing a crime or dying from a stress-related illness. The findings for the population as a whole suggest, however, that stress induced by economic conditions can lead to a shorter life, more illness, and increased aggression for those who are employed as well as the unemployed.

Besides discussing the human consequences of adverse economic performance, the results of Brenner's study can be used to estimate the dollar costs of increased pathology to society. While the calculations involved are necessarily approximate, they point to a wide range of direct and indirect costs associated with higher unemployment. Their magnitude should emphasize to policy makers the importance of keeping unemployment at a minimum.

In 1977, according to a recent study by Research Triangle Institute in North Carolina, the cost to society of problems related to alcohol, drug abuse and mental illness amounted to $106 billion.[8] This figure includes both direct expenditures on health care (in hospitals, clinics, and nursing homes, as well as physician's services and drugs) and an estimate of indirect costs—mainly the lost or reduced productivity of those who become ill. The latter measure attempts to value the goods and services (including unpaid household services) of which society has been deprived due to illness, disability, or death. While over $88 billion of the total is accounted for by the costs of medical care and forgone income, a variety of other factors—particularly in the case of drug abuse—are economically important: for example, the costs of crimes committed by drug addicts and concomitant expenditures by the criminal justice system.

For each of the pathologies considered in Brenner's study, similar cost estimates can be obtained. For example, heart attacks and strokes cost the nation $109 billion in medical services and forgone earnings of those afflicted. One year's homicide victims, according to a 1976 estimate of the Joint Economic Committee, would have earned $3.6 billion had they lived a normal lifespan. Of course, only a fraction of the cost in any of these cases can be attributable to economic factors. Based on the increments of additional pathology found by the study to be related to economic changes, an appropriate portion of the cost can be calculated.

Based on changes in unemployment, income, and other conditions in the mid-1970s, Brenner estimates dollar losses due to recession-related increases in mortality at $26 billion (see table 5–8). This reflects resources taken from productive use, which reduce the real wealth of our society.

This information leads to two major conclusions. The first is that changes in unemployment, real per capita income, and other measures of

Table 5–8
**Economic Loss due to Changes in Unemployment, per Capita Income, and the Business Failure Rate during 1973 and 1974**[a]
*(millions of 1980 dollars)*

| Social Stress Indicator | Representing Economic Cost of | Economic Loss |
|---|---|---|
| Total mortality | Total illness | 26,222 |
| Cardiovascular mortality | Diseases of the circulatory system | 15,950 |
| Population in mental hospitals | Hospitalization in state and county mental institutions | 495 |
| Suicide | Suicide | 31 |
| Total arrests | Criminal justice system | 1,970 |
| Arrests for fraud and embezzlement | White collar crime | 3,061 |
| Homicide | Homicide | 137 |

Source: M. Harvey Brenner, *Estimating the Effects of Economic Change on National Health and Social Well-Being*, Joint Economic Committee, Congress of the United States (Washington, D.C.: U.S. Government Printing Office, 1984), p. vi.
[a]Estimates are based on a 14.3 percent increase in the unemployment rate; a 3 percent decline in trend per capita income, and a 200 percent decline in trend per capita income, and a 200 percent increase in annual change in the business failure rate.

economic performance are correlated with crime, mortality, and a number of physical and mental illnesses. Secondly, a major deterioration of economic conditions such as that occurring during recession will have a pathological impact on hundreds of thousands of people, with a multibillion dollar cost to society. This cost will be experienced even after the contraction has ended.

## Summary

The contraction phase of the business cycle has a number of important economic effects. First, since actual output falls well below potential output, there is considerable economic waste as the economy produces at less than capacity level.

Not only is there a loss in terms of physical production, but there is considerable waste of human resources. The latter is associated with the increase in unemployment that inevitably accompanies a cyclical downturn.

Although all sectors of the labor force experience an increase in unemployment when the economy experiences a cyclical decline, certain industries and occupations are particularly hard hit. Durable goods producers, construction workers, and miners tend to have the largest absolute increases in unemployment rates during a recession.

The increased unemployment associated with recession (cyclical unemployment) has important indirect effects on health status. M. Harvey Brenner has shown that higher unemployment rates cause an increase in cardiovascular mortality, suicide, and admission to mental hospitals. His research implies that the stress associated with deteriorating economic conditions results in reduced lifespan, increased morbidity, and more aggressiveness for those who are employed and unemployed. The dollar cost to society associated with these higher incidences of pathology is in the billions.

## Notes

1. Edward F. Dennison, "The Interruption of Productivity Growth in the United States," *The Economic Journal* 93, no. 369 (March 1983): 56–77.

2. Edward F. Dennison, *Trends in American Economic Growth, 1929–1982*, The Brookings Institution, Washington, D.C., 1985), p. 4.

3. U.S. Department of Commerce, *Economic Report of the President, 1987* (Washington, D.C. U.S. Government Printing Office, 1987), p. 280.

4. Alan Sorkin, *Education, Unemployment and Economic Growth* (Cambridge, Mass.: D.C. Heath & Co., 1974), p. 10.

5. U.S. Department of Commerce, "The Business Situation," *Survey of Current Business*, December 1982, p. 7.

6. Ibid., p. 8.

7. M. Harvey Brenner, *Estimating the Social Costs of National Economic Policy: Implications for Mental and Physical Health and Criminal Aggression*, Paper no. 5, Joint Economic Committee, U.S. Congress, 1976, p. vii.

8. Cited in M. Harvey Brenner, *Estimating the Effects of Economic Change on National Health and Social Well-Being*, Joint Economic Committee, U.S. Congress (Washington, D.C.: U.S. Government Printing Office, 1984), p. v.

# 6
# Monetary Policy

The Federal Reserve System (the central banking system) plays a major institutional role in the development of macroeconomic policy. The primary function of the Federal Reserve is to control the supply of bank reserves and thus profoundly influence the quantity of money and credit in the economy.

The objectives of the Federal Reserve are price stability, strong economic growth, and low unemployment. If total aggregate demand is too great, so that the rate of inflation is increasing, the Federal Reserve Board may want to reduce the growth rate of the money supply. If unemployment is high and economic activity stagnant or declining, the Federal Reserve may increase the money supply in order to stimulate aggregate demand.

## Definitions of the Money Supply

There are two alternative definitions of the money supply, termed $M_1$ and $M_2$. $M_1$ is the supply of money that includes transactions accounts. This encompasses demand deposits (non-interest-earning checking accounts) at commercial banks and other deposits on which checks can be drawn. Demand deposits were traditionally the major component of $M_1$ besides currency, but $M_1$ now includes several types of "other checkable deposits." These include negotiated orders of withdrawal (NOW accounts) and "Super NOW" accounts at thrift institutions; automatic transfer system (ATS) accounts at commercial banks, permitting automatic transfers from savings accounts to cover overdrafts; and similar accounts at credit unions.

$M_2$ includes everything that is encompassed in $M_1$. In addition $M_2$ includes passbook savings accounts, as well as statement savings accounts that allow deposits and withdrawals to be made by mail. Other components of $M_2$ include money market accounts, money market mutual funds, repurchase orders and Eurodollar deposits. Savings certificates are also included in $M_2$ if they are less than \$100,000 in denomination. These certificates have varying dates of maturity, ranging from six months to several years, and either fixed or variable interest rates. The final component of $M_2$ consists of overnight repurchase agreements.

The original source of the distinction between $M_1$ and $M_2$ was that $M_1$ was limited to assets that could be used for exchange; that is, currency and checking accounts (demand deposits). Between the 1930s and the late 1970s the distinction between checking accounts and savings accounts was legally enforced by Federal Reserve regulations. Only checking accounts could be used for payments by check, and checking accounts paid no interest. Moreover, savings accounts could not be used for transactions purposes, but interest was paid on deposits.

Beginning in the late 1970s, however, banking regulations were changed in three ways. First, the Federal Reserve started to allow banks to pay interest on checking accounts. Second, banks were permitted to issue checkbooks for savings accounts.[1] Third, institutions other than banks and thrift institutions were allowed to offer money market mutual funds that issued checkbooks and paid interest. Occasionally they paid higher interest rates than banks paid on checking or savings accounts. By the mid 1980s, the distinction between checking accounts, savings accounts, and money market mutual funds had essentially disappeared. Each could be used for checks, and each paid interest at close to the short-term market interest rate. The only remaining differences were restrictions imposed by the banks and financial institutions on service charges and the minimum allowable size of a check.

## The Expansion or Contraction of Bank Deposits

The key concept for understanding changes in the money supply $(M_1)$ is the principle of fractional reserves. Generally a commercial bank need only keep a fraction of its total deposit liabilities on hand to meet withdrawals of deposits by its customers. Reserves not needed for this purpose are considered excess reserves and are available for the bank to use profitably by making additional loans. Any individual bank in the system is limited in its lending capability and hence, money-creating ability, by the amount of its excess reserves. For all banks together, the increase in the money supply through creation of new demand deposits is a multiple of the reserves banks are required to keep on hand to meet their obligations. The actual amount of reserves is determined by the Federal Reserve System. What is important to understand, however, is that the fractional reserve principle permits the commercial banking system to expand its deposit liabilities by some multiple of the total reserves in the system. It is this phenomenon that makes it appropriate to describe reserve money as "high-powered" money." Every dollar of reserve money can "create" through the banking system four or five dollars more of added demand deposit money.

If $X$ is the fraction of bank deposits that an individual bank must keep on reserve then $1/X$, the reciprocal of the required reserve ratio, can be termed the money multiplier. For example, if the required reserve ratio is .20 (20 percent), its reciprocal is 5 (the money multiplier). Consequently, every dollar of high-powered money in the system can support $5 in demand deposits.

It is through excess reserves that the central bank obtains its leverage over the nation's monetary system. By moving reserves into or out of the banking system it creates the necessary conditions for an expansion or contraction of the money supply. However, the Federal Reserve System cannot force an increase in the money supply. It can put more reserves into the banking system, but this does not mean that individuals and firms will increase the level of borrowing. Only if the latter occurs will demand deposits (and the money supply) increase. However, if the Federal Reserve pursues policies that lower commercial bank reserves, the latter will be forced to reduce their liabilities. This means they will call in loans and reduce the volume of new lending activity. These actions will result in a reduction in the money supply.

## Tools of Monetary Policy

The Federal Reserve's most important tool is "open-market operations." By selling or purchasing government securities in the open market, it is able to increase or decrease bank reserves. These so-called open-market operations are a central bank's most important method of economic stabilization.

Every month the Federal Open-Market Committee (FOMC) meets to determine whether to increase the level of bank reserves by buying Treasury bills (that is, short-term bonds) and longer-term government bonds (and concomitantly to lower interest rates), or whether to tighten monetary policy (raise interest rates) by selling government securities and thus decreasing the level of reserves.

Sometimes the Federal Reserve must engage in open-market operations even when it has no desire to raise or lower the money supply. For instance, during the Christmas shopping season, the public needs more cash for transactions. Without action by the Federal Reserve the money supply would be reduced. Banks would use some of their reserves to provide cash to the public and would have fewer reserves remaining to support deposits. Thus, the money supply would decline by a multiple of the public's cash withdrawals. The Federal Reserve can prevent this decline in the money supply from occurring by conducting a "defensive" open-market purchase of bonds. This action provides banks with the extra reserves that are required to handle the public's cash withdrawals.

## The Rediscount Rate

The Federal Reserve banks make loans to member banks. These loans can be termed *borrowed reserves*. When borrowed reserves are growing, the banks are borrowing from the Federal Reserve System, which is thereby helping total bank reserves to increase. When borrowed reserves are declining, that situation can result in a contraction of total bank reserves.

Banks decide how much to borrow from the Federal Reserve System by comparing the interest rate it is charging, the rediscount rate, with the interest rate the banks can receive by investing the funds received. Federal Reserve loans tend to be high when the interest rate on short-term investments, such as the interest rate on federal funds, is substantially above the system's rediscount rate.

Because $200 million in Federal Reserve loans provides banks with $200 million in additional bank reserves, as does a $200 million open-market purchase, the Federal Reserve can control high-powered money either by varying the rediscount rate or by conducting open-market operations. Monetary control can be achieved with either policy instrument and does not require both of them. The major justification for continuing the practice of lending by the Federal Reserve is the possible need for assistance by individual banks suffering from an unexpected increase in withdrawals. Such instances are uncommon, however, and could be handled on an individual basis. Many economists have criticized the Federal Reserve for continuing its lending policy, because when interest rates are high, it tends to keep its rediscount rate low enough to induce substantial borrowing by banks. This policy reduces the precision of the Federal Reserve's control (on a short-term basis) of the quantity of high-powered money.

## Reserve Requirements

The Federal Reserve can raise the money supply by reducing bank reserve requirements $(X)$, or it can reduce the money supply by increasing reserve requirements up to the 14 percent statutory limit on demand deposits.

While variations in reserve requirements are a potentially important monetary policy tool, changes are made only after a period of years, not on a daily basis the way open-market operations are employed. Reserve requirements are changed very infrequently, because it is a large and abrupt change in policy. Open-market operations can achieve the same results in a much less disruptive way.

The last time a major change in reserve requirements occurred was in 1980. The Federal Reserve and President Carter were concerned about excessive speculation in the commodity and financial markets. They imposed credit controls and raised reserve requirements. Speculation decreased but the recession that occurred from January to July 1980 can be partly attributed to this policy.

## The Timing and Impact of Monetary Policy

Although most changes in fiscal policy must be legislated by Congress, an important advantage of monetary policy is the short decision-making (legislative) lag as compared to fiscal policy. Once a majority of the Federal Open-Market Committee decides, for example, that an increase in the growth rate of money supply is appropriate, only a short period of time passes until the next FOMC meeting. (This group comes together once a month.) If the FOMC has decided to engage in open-market purchases, the expansion in the rate of growth of the money supply begins almost immediately, although the full impact of this money creation process may require one or two months (transmission lag).

Most of the controversy about the lag in terms of monetary policy concerns the length of time before a policy change has an impact on real output and employment (the effectiveness lag). Friedman described this lag as both long and variable.[2] Gordon estimated this lag in monetary policy for the last six postwar recessions. The average effectiveness lag was 7.8 months, the shortest being 5 months (the 1980 recession) and the longest 10 months (the 1957–1958 and 1973–1975 recessions).[3]

Aside from the problem of lags, another issue is the distributional impact of monetary policy. For example, a large corporation often has adequate financial reserves, and thus may have no need to borrow from the loanable funds market in order to obtain capital for expansion or to meet unexpected current expenses. The small firm, however, has fewer internal financing resources and is more dependent on bank credit to finance some of its activities. In a period of tight money, the effects of monetary policy may fall most heavily on small businesses, leaving large firms relatively unaffected by central bank policies. Since the spending decisions of large corporations generally have more impact on the economy than those of small businesses, some of the effectiveness of monetary policy may be lost. Moreover, industrial concentration—the tendency for an industry to be dominated by a small number of major producers—is encouraged by a tight money policy.

In addition, different investment expenditures vary a great deal in their responsiveness to the rate of interest. For example, expenditures for buildings, including residential housing, are much more sensitive to a change in

Table 6–1
Interest Rates and New Housing, 1965–1986

| Year | Mortgage Rates ((percent) | Housing Starts (thousands of units) |
|------|---------------------------|-------------------------------------|
| 1965 | 5.81 | 1,473 |
| 1966 | 6.25 | 1,165 |
| 1967 | 6.46 | 1,292 |
| 1968 | 6.97 | 1,508 |
| 1969 | 7.81 | 1,467 |
| 1970 | 8.45 | 1,433 |
| 1971 | 7.74 | 2,052 |
| 1972 | 7.60 | 2,357 |
| 1973 | 7.95 | 2,045 |
| 1974 | 8.92 | 1,338 |
| 1975 | 9.01 | 1,160 |
| 1976 | 8.99 | 1,538 |
| 1977 | 9.02 | 1,987 |
| 1978 | 9.56 | 2,020 |
| 1979 | 10.78 | 1,745 |
| 1980 | 12.66 | 1,292 |
| 1981 | 15.14 | 1,062 |
| 1983 | 12.57 | 1,703 |
| 1984 | 12.38 | 1,750 |
| 1985 | 11.55 | 1,741 |
| 1986 | 10.17 | 1,806 |

Source: U.S. Department of Commerce, *Economic Report of the President,* 1987 (Washington, D.C.: U.S. Government Printing Office, 1987), p. 302 and 324.

the rate of interest than are business expenditures for inventories or even new equipment. Table 6–1 indicates mortgage interest rates and new (private) housing starts for the twenty-two year period 1965 through 1986. Note the sharp downturn in new housing construction in the years of tight money (reduced credit availability and high interest rates)—1966, 1969, 1973–1975 and 1980–1982. Thus, a stringent monetary policy leading to a sharp rise in the rate of interest affects investment spending unevenly. It is debatable that such a distributional impact is socially desirable.

## Monetary Policy, 1956–1961

During 1956 the growth in nominal $M_1$ was slow and the real money supply fell. Interest rates rose as output increased. In 1957 the growth rate of total output began to decline partly because of the tight money policy followed during the previous year. Instead of adopting an easier monetary policy to stimulate the growth of output, the Federal Reserve policy became more restrictive. This resulted in a decline in both the nominal and real money supply ($M_1$), thus aggravating the sharp 1957–1958 recession.

This same mistake was made in 1959–1960. In early 1960 the Federal Reserve allowed both the nominal and real money supply ($M_1$) to decline even though the economy was characterized by considerable excess capacity. This restrictive policy made the 1960–1961 recession more severe than would have been the case if an easy money policy had been pursued. The timing and magnitude of the 1960–1961 recession may have played a role in the defeat of Richard Nixon by John Kennedy in the presidential election.

During this period the Federal Reserve failed to follow a countercyclical monetary policy, pursuing a procyclical policy instead. In defense of these actions one should note that during the 1956–1961 period the Federal Reserve was concerned about keeping the rate of inflation moderate. This concern was reflected in a tight monetary policy during the expansion phase of the cycle, when inflationary pressures would be greatest.

## Monetary Policy, 1964–1971

At this time the Federal Reserve followed a procyclical monetary policy on two occasions. During both 1965–1966 and 1967–1968, it permitted both the nominal and real money supply to accelerate even though the economy had returned to full employment by 1965. Excessive monetary growth throughout this period was one major reason why the rate of growth in consumer prices rose from 1.0 percent in 1964 to about 5 percent by 1970. The accelerated pace of inflation contributed to the steady rise in both short- and long-term interest rates.

During 1964–1971, a tight money policy was twice undertaken. The first time was during a six-month period in 1966, and the second was over a fifteen-month period in 1969–1970. The first period of monetary tightness had little impact on overall economic activity, but the second contributed to the 1969–1970 recession. Why was there such a difference in the policy impact?

The later period lasted nearly 2½ times as long as the first, permitting a greater cumulative impact on the economy. Moreover, in 1966–1967 fiscal policy had clearly been stimulative as U.S. involvement in the Vietnam War was steadily increasing and the level of government expenditures was rising. By 1969–1970, however, our participation in Vietnam was declining and the impact of the 1968 tax surcharge also indicated that fiscal policy had become restrictive.

## Monetary Policy, 1971–79

As a generalization monetary policy helped contribute to the instability of the economy during the decade of the 1970s. The very rapid growth in the real money supply during 1972 was associated with the speculative excesses and rapid inflation that characterized the latter stages of the 1971–1973 boom period.

In early 1974 total output fell in response to supply limitations associated with the shortage of oil and a reduction in food production. Inflation worsened partly because of the above shortages and the removal of price controls. Because of concern with inflation, monetary policy become restrictive, which pushed up interest rates and made the recession longer and deeper than would have been the case if a countercyclical monetary policy had been followed.

The optimal countercyclical monetary policy to encourage a rapid recovery from the 1973–1975 recession would have been rapid $M_1$ growth in 1975–1976, when actual output was far below potential output and unemployment was high. This should have been followed by a gradual retardation in the rate of monetary growth in 1977–1978 as the economic recovery became more vigorous. The Federal Reserve policy, however, allowed $M_1$ growth to accelerate steadily as the economy recovered. This contributed to the very high rates of inflation in 1978, 1979, and 1980.

## Monetarism and Money Supply Targeting

Monetarism is a school of macroeconomic thought that emphasizes the importance of competition and flexible wages and prices as the determinants of aggregate output and employment, and of the money supply as the determinant of the price level. Monetarists generally accept the classical view that a competitive market economy will only be in long-run equilibrium at the level of full employment.

In general monetarists oppose an active role for the government in regulating aggregate demand by varying the rate of growth of the money supply. If the economy reaches long-run equilibrium only at the full employment level of aggregate output, then aggregate demand and the money supply only affect prices and the rate of inflation in the long run and have no impact on total output or employment. Monetarists also maintain that because of the existence of the policy lags discussed above, the size or timing of the effects of money supply changes are unknown. Since the timing and impact of lags are uncertain, the monetary authorities may, for example, increase the rate of growth of the money supply to stimulate demand during a recession, but the expansionary effects may not occur until the contraction is over. In this situation the monetary authorities could simply worsen inflationary pressures during a period of strong economic growth.

Given the lack of success of the Federal Reserve in pursuing a counter-cyclical monetary policy, monetarists advocate monetary rules to reduce the discretion of the monetary authorities to change the rate of growth of the money supply. One of the most common of the monetarist rules is to determine a constant annual rate of growth of the money supply over a period of time. The constant rate would be tied to the long-term trends in the growth of real GNP and the velocity of money.[4]

## Targeting

In the late 1970s, the Federal Reserve began to realize that its traditional procedures put too much relative emphasis on interest rate stability resulting in a procyclical movement in the growth of the money supply. In October 1979 the Federal Reserve Board shifted from a policy of short-term monetary control to direct control of *nonborrowed reserves*. Bank reserves are a major component of high-powered money. Nonborrowed reserves are equal to total bank reserves minus bank borrowings from the Federal Reserve.

It was expected that this change in procedures would approximate a constant growth rate rule for the money supply as the monetarists had long advocated.

With the Federal Reserve's primary emphasis on controlling $M_1$ and less on controlling the interest rate, there was a major increase in the volatility of short-term interest rates between 1980 and 1982. One commentator described the effects of the 1980–1982 experience as "virtual bedlam."[5]

Fluctuations in the federal funds rate not only became larger but also spread faster to other short-term rates and to long-term interest rates—particularly the rates on long-term government bonds. The long-term interest rate volatility translated into greater price volatility of long-term bonds and thus exposed traders to greater financial risk. Because many traders were unwilling to take this risk, the number of participants in the bond market declined, and interest rate volatility was exacerbated. Other traders increased the markup of their selling price over the buying price, thus raising costs for those attempting to raise funds via the bond market.

Not only was this period characterized by extreme interest rate volatility, but during the time the Federal Reserve was following a highly restrictive policy (particulary from late 1979 to mid-1981) interest rates rose to unprecedented levels. The high level of interest rates during 1981 and early

1982 was partially responsible for the severity of the 1981–1982 recession.

Although, as indicated above, the Federal Reserve System established money supply targets during 1979–1982, it frequently exceeded them by large margins. This was partly because the system still followed some of its traditional operating procedures. For example, it continued to attempt to smooth weekly and monthly fluctuations in interest rates, and it was prepared to allow the growth rate of the money supply to deviate from its stated target if the Federal Reserve believed that was necessary to help offset a particular movement in interest rates. Moreover, it allowed the target zones for successive years to drift away from the path for the money supply that had originally been intended.

Between 1979 and 1981 the Federal Reserve monetary policy was unfortunately as procyclical as it had been in previous recessions. Thus, from January 1980 until mid-1982 real $M_1$ declined at the same time as real output and employment fell.

## The Changing Regulatory Structure

The first modification was to separate transactions accounts from nontransactions accounts. A transactions account is one (like currency or checking accounts) whose primary purpose is to serve as a means of payment. A nontransactions account is an asset (like a savings account) whose primary purpose is to put aside funds for the future, as opposed to being used to pay bills. Of course, the distinction between these two categories is not perfectly clear, but the difference remained until the 1980s.

Once this separation was made, the 1980 and 1982 Banking Acts effectively deregulated nontransactions accounts. The legislation required interest rate ceilings to be phased out by 1986.[6] Moreover, the reserve requirements on these deposits are essentially zero. These kinds of deposits pay market interest rates and fall outside the direct influence of Federal Reserve policies. The remaining assets—the transactions assets like checking accounts—have only been partially deregulated. Since 1986, they have no longer been subject to interest rate ceilings, but they continue to be subject to substantial reserve requirements (around 12 percent of total deposits).

No one knows exactly what the long-term effect of these regulatory changes will be. Many economists believe that the Federal Reserve has had a more difficult time controlling the economy since deregulation has occurred. The money supply has behaved more erratically and the Federal Reserve, as discussed above, has found achieving its monetary targets a difficult task.

A problem for those who formulate monetary policy is the variability of the demand for money or its velocity. Previous research on this matter tended to support the view that the velocity of money was relatively stable, or at least predictable by forecasting models. More recent work casts doubt on this conclusion. Before 1982 velocity had been increasing, and the demand for money falling. In 1982 and 1983, however, velocity fell sharply, which is to say, the demand for money increased. The major reason usually given for the observed variation in velocity is the growth in substitutes for money and associated structural and regulatory changes in the financial services industry.[7] A second explanation for the unpredictability of velocity is the degree of uncertainty due to the volatility of the money supply and interest rates. Thus, with growing uncertainty, the public would prefer to have more cash on hand, thus reducing velocity.

## The Disinflation of the 1980s

Monetary policy does not solely focus on moderating fluctuations in economic activity. It is also concerned with reducing the rate of inflation when appropriate.

Many analysts date the recent determination to reduce inflation in the United States to October 1979, when the Federal Reserve announced a change in its operating procedures to achieve more direct control of the money supply. $M_1$ growth fluctuated widely in 1980 and showed no sustained deceleration until 1981. Despite this short-term variability, the trend rate of money growth (measured as the annual rate of change over eight quarters) fell from 8.4 percent in the third quarter of 1979 to 6.3 percent three years later. This monetary deceleration provided the initial impetus for disinflation. Inflation in 1982, as measured by the consumer price index (CPI), was less than half the 1980 rate and by 1983 had been reduced to less than one-fourth the 1980 rate. Thus, the decline in inflation was greater than would have been implied by the decline in the trend of money growth.[8]

The shift to a disinflationary monetary policy probably contributed to an appreciation of the value of the dollar that began in mid-1980 (see chapter 7). In the short run, this has helped to hold down prices of imported goods but has resulted in additional price competition for many domestically produced goods and worsened the balance of payments deficit. After decontrol, domestic crude oil prices (measured by the producer price index) fell more than 21 percent from the end of 1981 to the end of 1985, and the energy products component of the CPI has registered very modest increases during that period.[9] In addition, deregulation in some industries, such as transportation and telecommunications, has likely caused relative price declines. All these relative price adjustments probably had some favorable effect on the observed inflation rate, holding it temporarily below the rate implied by long-term money growth.

In some cases individual prices have actually declined in recent years. The index of raw commodities spot prices has, for example, declined 26 percent from 1980 to 1985; prices of some commodities are down as much as 40 to 50 percent. In each case, however, these relative price declines do not constitute deflation, anymore than the nearly 34 percent increase in the price of medical care services since 1982 constitutes rapid inflation.[10] While relative price changes have helped reduce the observed inflation rate in recent years, as long as the overall consumer price index continues to rise— although much more slowly—generalized inflation continues.

Disinflationary policies were adopted on three separate occasions before 1981. During 1969–1970 and in 1974–1975 money growth was reduced substantially, and after a lag of $1\frac{1}{2}$ to 2 years inflation also declined. In addition, $M_1$ growth fell in late 1979 and early 1980 but accelerated during the second half of the year. In all three instances, a recession was associated with the occurrence of disinflationary monetary policy. In theory it may be possible to devise a monetary policy strategy that would reduce inflation without necessarily also resulting in a contraction. However, in reality, restrictive monetary policy in the United States, as well as in other countries, has frequently been associated with a decline in real economic activity. This is often the major long-run cost of a rise in inflation.

Moreover, to the extent that expectations of inflation are built into financial contracts, the effects of a disinflationary policy will remain for a considerable period after the actual inflation rate has declined. Many of the credit market and other financial problems of the mid-1980s were basically related to the inflation-disinflation process. The rise in the inflation rate in the 1970s provided a strong incentive to incur indebtedness. The tax deduction for interest expense made this position financially attractive. Assumption of debt is a reasonable strategy in a high-inflation environment, but it leaves both creditors and borrowers vulnerable to an unexpected abatement of inflationary pressure. In the agriculture, real estate, and energy sectors, for example, debt was assumed (in the late 1970s) on the expectation that real asset values and some commodity prices would continue to rise at rapid rates. Much of the credit extended to less-developed countries (LDCs) when inflation was high was made on the assumption that energy and raw materials prices would continue to increase rapidly enough to generate the foreign exchange earnings these countries needed to service the debt. Subsequently, repayment problems arose when the actual inflation rate fell below expectations.

In the late 1970s and in 1980 those who borrowed money at fixed interest rates benefited as inflation rates rose faster than expectations. A substantial part of their gain came at the expense of creditors and holders of fixed-rate financial assets. Later, when inflation declined more rapidly than anticipated, borrowers' real debt-service burdens increased. Thus the debt problems in various sectors, as well as the associated stress in some financial institutions, are related to the market valuation of real assets and outstanding debt in a disinflationary environment. In addition, debt contin-ued to be assumed and credit extended on the assumption of high inflation even as the rate of inflation was declining. The failure of inflationary expectations to decline as the inflation rate fell after 1981, therefore, pro-longed the period of adjustment and worsened the debt problems in some sectors of the economy.

## The "Optimal" Disinflation Policy

Although economists generally agree that reducing inflation requires a de-cline in the trend of money growth, there is much less agreement regarding the best way to achieve disinflation. Some negative real and financial effects are almost inevitable, but it is not clear what set of policies or rate of disinflation is most likely to minimize economic disruption. It is possible, however, to identify some aspects of a disinflationary policy that would be expected to ease the adjustment process and limit the resultant economic dislocation.

Once the expectation of continued high inflation is built into economic institutions and behavior, the transition to disinflation requires that expec-tations and behavior be changed. Economic costs—in lost jobs and output—are incurred when private behavior that is adapted to an in-flationary environment confronts a disinflationary monetary policy.

As mentioned earlier, inflation was temporarily reduced in two separate periods during the 1970s, then allowed to reaccelerate each time to a rate higher than the previous peak. This probably contributed to public skepti-cism about the government's ability or willingness to control inflation over the long run. The monetary events of 1980 may have added to this doubt. Money growth declined in late 1979 and early 1980, and the money supply declined absolutely after credit controls were imposed in March 1980. Interest rates fell sharply, as did the short-term inflation rate as output fell rapidly in the second quarter of 1980. All these developments were abruptly reversed after mid-1980, however, as money growth, interest rates, and inflation all soared to growth rates exceeding 10 percent. The extreme volatility of macroeconomic policy and the associated variability in interest rates and the inflation rate likely increased economic uncertainty gener-ally.[11]

Stable, well-publicized policies that are consistent with the stated goal of lower inflation can facilitate the downward adjustment of expectations regarding the rate of inflation. This is true for fiscal as well as monetary policy. In contrast, when policy goals are vague, and short-term actions are unpredictable or inconsistent with long-term goals, adjustment of expectations is likely to be slowed and the economic cost of reducing inflation is likely to be increased.

The Reagan administration recommended in 1981 that money growth be decelerated in a gradual and predictable pattern. Such a disinflationary monetary policy would have allowed time for the public to recognize and accept the changes and to adjust inflation expectations and behavior accordingly.

Regardless of intentions, it is difficult to characterize the deceleration of money growth in 1981–1982 as either gradual or predictable. The administration's objective was a gradual reduction in money supply growth to 3 percent per annum in 1986. In fact, more than half of the deceleration in money growth that the administration had expected to occur over a six-year period was actually realized during 1981. Moreover, there were two six-month periods during 1981 and early 1982 when $M_1$ growth was negligible. As a result of the substantial slowdown in monetary growth, inflation probably fell more rapidly than it otherwise would have. As noted previously, the abrupt reduction in $M_1$ growth, as well as the protracted periods of very slow money growth, probably contributed to the duration and depth of the 1981–1982 recession.

Moreover, in spite of the new targeting policy, the variability of $M_1$ growth actually increased substantially after 1979; the standard deviation of quarterly $M_1$ growth increased from 2.2 percent in the six-year period preceding October 1979 to 4.8 percent in the six-year period thereafter. During the seven-quarter period of decelerated money growth that began in 1981, for example, quarterly growth rates of $M_1$ ranged from 3.0 to 9.2 percent. This is considerably more variability in $M_1$ growth than can be attributed to the technical limitations of monetary control.[12]

In the context of relatively stable prices, such monetary volatility might not be particularly important. However, in the early 1980s a major challenge facing policy makers was to restore policy credibility. In that environment, each reacceleration of money growth encouraged the belief that disinflationary policy was only temporary and thereby helped maintain and reinforce inflationary expectations even as the actual inflation rate fell substantially.

Uncertainty about future inflation may also have been worsened by the emergence of large budget deficits (see chapter 7). Large current and prospective budget deficits tend to increase expectations that the Federal Reserve will ultimately increase the growth rate of the money supply and thereby generate higher inflation, which would ease the burden of accumulated debt. Concerns about the budget deficit, therefore, may have interacted with the uncertainty caused by volatile money growth, resulting in a major impediment to the downward adjustment of inflationary expectations.

## Monetary Policy, 1981–1984

There were three major phases to monetary policy over the 1981–1984 period. In the first phase, extending to mid-1982, the Federal Reserve's main concern was to restore credibility in the markets by pursuing a restrictive monetary policy designed to reduce inflation. Although the 1980 credit control program was a contributing factor, monetary policy procedures introduced in October 1979 quite generally yielded *both* volatile interest rates and volatile money growth. Moreover, as the recession developed, the average rate of money growth in 1981 and the first half of 1982 was substantially lower than it had been over the previous several years. As stated previously, money growth did not decline gradually and predictably as advocated by the Reagan administration, but declined sharply.

The second phase of monetary policy began in the late summer of 1982. Prompted by the international debt crisis and increasing evidence that the recession would be deeper and longer lasting than had been predicted, the Federal Reserve abandoned the short-run operating procedures (targeting) introduced in October 1979 and turned to procedures that involved more flexible targets.[13]

Interest rates fell sharply as money growth accelerated beginning in August 1982. The Federal Reserve permitted money growth to remain high as deregulation allowed depository institutions to introduce new types of deposit accounts in December 1982 and January 1983, making temporarily difficult the interpretation of the monetary aggregates data. However, as the economy improved in the winter and spring of 1983, both the Federal Reserve and the administration became quite concerned about the continuing high rate of money growth.

The third phase of monetary policy began in the late spring of 1983. Controlling money growth again became an important objective of Federal Reserve policy, and interest rates were permitted to rise. From the middle of 1983 through mid-1984, money growth was substantially below the rate from mid-1982 to mid-1983. In the second half of 1984, the rate of money growth declined even further.

### Review of 1981–1984 Economic Performance

Shortly after this administration took office it was faced with a recession. At the end of 1981 and into early 1982, however, there were reasons to believe that the recession would not be particularly deep. In 1982 the *initially* reported data showed that in the first quarter real final sales grew at a 1.9 percent annual rate—the data were subsequently revised to indicate a decline of 1.0 percent—and that in the second quarter real GNP rose at a 1.7 percent rate—the data were revised to indicate a decline of 0.8 percent. Thus, later in the year new information indicated that the economy was weaker than had been thought.

Late 1982 was a very difficult time for economic forecasters and policy makers. Although the usual signs of recovery were accumulating, many observers remained pessimistic. However, by the end of 1982 the recession was over. The unemployment rate peaked at 10.8 percent in November and December. By early 1983, the probable resumption of economic growth was signaled by a number of indicators including growth in real final sales that rose at a 5.5 percent annual rate in the fourth quarter of 1982. With final sales rising while total output declined slowly, there was a substantial reduction of inventories, which helped to provide the conditions for a resumption of output growth.[14]

It appears that the changing velocity of money contributed to the depth of the recession. Money demand—measured by the quantity of money held relative to GNP—rose to an unusual degree, probably reflecting both the reduced cost of holding money balances as market interest rates fell and the spread of interest-bearing negotiable order of withdrawal (NOW) accounts nationwide. Uncertainty attributable to volatile economic and financial conditions may also have raised the demand for money. In addition, from early 1981 through mid-1982 the Federal Reserve permitted substantially lower $M_1$ money growth than had prevailed over the previous several years. This also resulted in downward pressure on the economy.

## Monetary Policy, 1985–1986

As discussed above, uncertainty about $M_1$ velocity behavior in recent years has made the formulation of monetary policy more difficult. Many observers have asserted that abnormal velocity behavior means that $M_1$ is no longer a useful target for monetary policy. While the trend growth of velocity and its interest elasticity may have been permanently altered, neither change would render $M_1$ permanently unreliable as a policy target. Moreover, the variables commonly suggested as alternatives to $M_1$—such as nominal and real interest rates, commodity prices, or the broader monetary aggregates—have important weaknesses as objectives for policy. The drawbacks of these alternatives are that either the Federal Reserve has limited control over them or their relationship to economic activity is difficult to predict.

The Federal Reserve followed an easy money policy in 1985 as interest rates fell, the dollar depreciated, and money growth was rapid. The Federal Reserve's actions were apparently motivated by a perceived need to foster stronger real economic growth. As mentioned earlier, efforts to adjust monetary policy to current economic conditions run the risk of being destabilizing. Because of the length and variability of the lags and inaccuracies in the initial reporting of some economic data, policy actions aimed at a currently perceived problem will not affect the economy until well after the problem has appeared and perhaps been eliminated. A policy of targeting real economic activity increases the probability that the policy itself becomes destabilizing as economic developments emerge that are unanticipated or inaccurately predicted.

In 1986, monetary policy was influenced by a wide range of economic and financial market developments. In the first four months of 1986, market interest rates declined substantially as the oil price declines and other price developments had favorable effects on the short-term outlook for inflation. In this period, the Federal Reserve Board reduced the discount rate twice in order to make it consistent with lower market interest rates. Money growth was relatively modest early in the year as $M_1$ expanded along the upper boundary of its target range and the broader aggregates were within or below their prescribed ranges. As evidence of economic weakness emerged in the second quarter and inflation remained very low (about 1 percent per annum), the Federal Open-Market Committee (FOMC) voted in July to ease reserve conditions and the Federal Reserve Board approved another cut in the discount rate, largely in response to additional downward movements in market interest rates that had occurred in June. Even though $M_1$ growth accelerated rapidly beginning in the spring, this policy action was considered appropriate by the administration because the broader monetary supply measures remained within their target ranges and uncertainty continued about the reliability of the linkage between $M_1$ and nominal income growth.

Similar policy actions were adopted again in August 1986 as economic activity continued to appear sluggish and the broader aggregates still grew at moderate rates, despite very rapid $M_1$ growth. Because each of the discount rate cuts in 1986 occurred after general declines in market interest rates, the discount rate followed, rather than led, interest rate movements.

By the summer of 1986, the broader monetary aggregates were also growing more rapidly and $M_2$ reached the upper bound of its target range in August. The FOMC appeared to become more concerned about the inflationary potential of money growth, a concern that had been apparently absent earlier in the year when $M_1$ alone was growing rapidly. Implicit in these decisions was the judgment that with the uncertainty about $M_1$ velocity, the broader monetary aggregates were considered more reliable guides to monetary policy than $M_1$. From the fourth quarter of 1985 to the fourth quarter of 1986, $M_1$ growth averaged more than 15 percent, well above the Federal Reserve's target range of 3 to 8 percent. $M_2$ growth from the fourth quarter of 1985 to the fourth quarter of 1986 was just at the upper bound of its 6 to 9 percent target range.[15]

As the economy expanded more slowly than expected during the year and inflation continued to be moderate, the Federal Reserve allowed $M_1$ growth to exceed its predefined target range and relied more heavily on a broader range of economic data. Further depreciation of the dollar in 1986 was apparently not interpreted as a signal of the need for slower money growth, probably because real dollar depreciation was widely regarded as desirable to improve U.S. international competitiveness, and because the lower dollar had little visible effect on the inflation rate. In the context of moderate real economic growth, very low inflation, and falling inflation expectations and given the uncertainty about the behavior of velocity, the deemphasis of $M_1$ in favor of other variables to gauge the conduct of monetary policy appears to have been an appropriate judgment.

Despite weaker-than-expected economic growth in 1986, no evidence suggests that the Federal Reserve has pursued an overly restrictive monetary policy. Based on money growth, interest rates, or exchange rates, it is not reasonable to conclude that monetary policy was "too tight" in 1986. The failure of the real economy to grow as rapidly as most forecasters had predicted is clearly related to sectoral problems and is not the result of inadequate monetary expansion. In particular, the adverse effects on the energy sector of the oil price declines, the further deterioration of the trade balance, and the continued weakness in the agricultural sector together appear to have limited economic growth in 1986.

One cannot ignore the fact that by historical standards, $M_1$ growth in 1986 was high. It substantially exceeded the Federal Reserve's own target range, as well as most analysts' views of appropriate money growth. Until a more reliable relationship between $M_1$ and nominal income growth is reestablished, however, the implications of this rapid $M_1$ growth will be unclear.

## Summary

Monetary policy is under the control of the Federal Reserve System. The Federal Reserve's main function is to exercise control of the level of bank reserves. Actions such as open-market sales or purchases, raising or lowering the rediscount rate, and reducing or increasing the level of required reserves will affect the supply of money and ultimately the level of economic activity.

The United States has two major definitions of the money supply. $M_1$ includes currency, demand deposits, and travelers checks. $M_2$ comprises $M_1$

and other assets, including savings deposits and certificates, repurchase orders, Eurodollar deposits, money market deposit accounts, and money market mutual funds.

Before the late 1970s, interest was not paid on checking accounts. However, between 1978 and 1985 several types of new accounts were introduced that allowed interest to be paid and checks to be written on the same account. The era of financial deregulation contributed to the instability in the demand for money partly because of the growth in substitutes for money.

Beginning in the late 1970s the Federal Reserve System began establishing targets for the growth of the major monetary aggregates ($M_1$ and $M_2$). By neglecting its traditional concern with the level of interest rates, this policy resulted in extraordinarily high interest rates in 1980 and 1981. This "strict targeting" policy contributed to the severity of the 1980 and 1981–1982 recessions. Since that initial experience with monetary targeting, the Federal Reserve has become more flexible, expressing its targets in ranges instead of precise amounts.

A number of factors may have effectively raised the cost of reducing inflation during the early 1980s. First the abrupt and unexpected decline in money supply growth in 1980–1982 probably made the 1981–1982 recession longer and more severe than would have been the case if a more gradual and predictable deceleration in money supply growth had occurred. Second, the slow adjustment of inflation expectations kept nominal interest rates high relative to the actual inflation rate. The public's reluctance to lower its expectations regarding the rate of inflation reflects the changing and unpredictable nature of monetary policy, large budget deficits, and the poor record of reduction in the rate of inflation during the 1970s.

Since 1981 there has been a considerable decline in the velocity of money. The changing regulatory structure and declines in interest rates and expected inflation are partially responsible for decreases in the velocity of money. Sharp changes in the velocity of money made countercyclical monetary policy hard to implement in 1981–1982 because these declines in velocity affected the supply of money.

Between 1957 and 1982 the Federal Reserve followed a procyclical monetary policy by permitting the real money supply to decline when the economy was weak and by accelerating monetary growth when the economy was strong.

## Notes

1. Robert Gordon, *Macroeconomics*, 4th ed. (Boston: Little Brown & Co., 1987), p. 389.

2. Milton Friedman and Anna Schwarz, *A Monetary History of the United*

*States, 1867–1960* (Princeton, N.J.: Princeton University Press, 1963).

3. Gordon, op. cit., p. 422.

4. Milton Friedman, "The Role of Monetary Policy," *American Economic Review* 58, no. 1 (March, 1968): 16.

5. Irving Overback, "Comment on Federal Reserve Policy, Interest Rate Volalility, and the U.S. Capital Raising Mechanism, Part 2," *Journal of Money, Credit and Banking* 14 (November 1982): 761–67.

6. U.S. Department of Commerce, *Economic Report of the President, 1987* (Washington, D.C.: U.S. Government Printing Office, 1987), p. 51.

7. Ibid., p. 52.

8. U.S. Department of Commerce, *Economic Report of the President, 1986* (Washington, D.C.: U.S. Government Printing Office, 1986), p. 30.

9. Ibid.

10. Ibid., p. 30.

11. Ibid., p. 35.

12. Ibid., p. 36.

13. U.S. Department of Commerce, *Economic Report of the President, 1985* (Washington, D.C.: U.S. Government Printing Office, 1985), p. 26.

14. Ibid., p. 28.

15. U.S. Department of Commerce, *1987*, op. cit., pp. 54–55.

# 7
# Fiscal Policy

F iscal policy is the process of deploying taxation and public expenditure programs in order to reduce the fluctuations of the business cycle and to contribute toward the achievement of economic growth, low unemployment, and reasonably stable price levels.

## The Automatic Stabilizers

The term stabilizers is utilized because these policy instruments (taxes and transfer payments) function in a manner that offsets fluctuations in economic activity. They are built in or automatic because they impact on the macroeconomic system without the making of specific policy decisions.

For example, taxes may serve to stabilize the economic system if the amount of taxes raised by the government rises with an increase in aggregate income. In this situation the effect will be to lessen the gain in disposable income that accompanies any autonomous upward shift in the aggregate demand function. From the standpoint of stabilization the consequence of this will be a slower rise in induced consumption spending than would occur with a tax system lacking this feature. If the tax system is progressive (higher tax rates for upper income recipients), the stabilizing impact will be even greater. This is because the effective rate at which income is taxed rises as the level of income increases. The stabilizing process operates in a reverse manner when the level of income declines. Thus, the fiscal system operates in a countercyclical or stabilizing direction when it is able partially to insulate disposable income from changes in national income.

The stabilizing effects of taxes depend on stable price levels: rapid inflation can cause the stabilizers to work in a perverse manner. One of the problems associated with the high inflation of the 1970s was that it moved many families into a higher tax bracket even though their current income was not rising more rapidly than the price level. Thus, the combination of inflation and a progressive tax structure caused a decline in real income for many families and individuals. Many economists believe that a major cause of the 1973–1975 recession was the decline in real income of consumers brought on by high inflation.

Thus far, the discussion of automatic stabilizers has focused on taxes, but transfer expenditures such as food stamps and unemployment insurance affect the economy in a similar countercyclical manner. For transfer payments to function as automatic stabilizers they must decrease in absolute amount when aggregate income rises and increase when total income falls. Consider, for example, the case of unemployment compensation payments. When output and employment are falling, payments to the unemployed automatically increase, thus moderating the decline in disposable income as well as net national product. When unemployment declines, such a during recovery from a recession or depression, transfer payments decline and thus disposable income rises more slowly than would be the case if the level of transfer payments remained constant.

The behavior of the automatic stabilizers over the course of the business cycle has been studied by a number of economists. One major study concluded that on the average a decline in national income resulted in a rise in transfer payments and a decline in tax revenues amounting to "a swing of approximately 50 percent of the decline in national income."[1]

Moreover, during business cycle upswings "the automatic stabilizers have exhibited a swing to increase of national income of slightly less than 30 percent on the average."[2] In other words, assuming a $10 billion increase in national income, disposable income will rise by about $3 billion less than would have been the case in the absence of automatic stabilizers.

## Discretionary Fiscal Policy

Even after automatic stabilizers have accomplished their purpose, fluctuations in economic activity remain. The principal tools of discretionary fiscal policy are public works and other government expenditure programs and tax rates.

One of the practical problems that inhibits the usefulness of discretionary fiscal policy is that it is frequently subject to long delays between the time the project or program is first proposed and the period when it has achieved its complete effect.

First, because both Congress and the president must approve changes in tax rates and/or government spending programs, long delays may occur between the time legislation is initially introduced by Congress until it is signed into law by the president. For example, President Johnson's economic advisors recognized in early 1966 the necessity for a tax increase to offset the potentially inflationary effects of increased government expenditures associated with the Vietnam War. The president postponed seeking a tax increase until after the 1966 congressional elections. Furthermore, Congress delayed passage of the tax increase for an additional eighteen months.

Although a change in tax rates can affect disposable income in a very short period of time, public works expenditures may take a year or two from the time they are first designed or developed, competitive bids are considered, and contracts are written until the project is actually begun.[3] It has been suggested that to minimize this delay an inventory of public works projects be developed that can be utilized in the event of a recession. Such a public works inventory has never existed. One objection to the idea is that, given the contractual nature of this work, it is not feasible to terminate partially completed projects if prosperity should return.

There is uncertainty regarding the length of time required after additional expenditures are first injected into the economic system until the ultimate effect on current GNP is obtained. For example, in the first three months following a $1-billion increase in government spending, estimates of the increase in current GNP range from $0.7 to $1.8 billion. After nine months have passed the estimates vary between $1.2 and $2.7 billion.[4]

Lower tax rates have frequently been used to stimulate the economy during a period of recession or slow growth. Once the legislation is approved, payroll deductions can be changed very quickly. The Barro-Ricardo equivalence-theorem, however, predicts that tax cuts will not significantly raise aggregate demand but instead will be offset by extra saving.[5] Changes in personal income tax rates in 1964, 1968, and 1975, for example, were largely negated by offsetting changes in personal saving.[6] This implies that consumption seems to be more a function of *permanent* income as compared to current income. The data for the 1981–1984 are not consistent with earlier findings. Recent tax cuts have not resulted in higher savings rates, but have clearly translated into increased demand.

Changes in government spending are more efficient than changes in tax rates because in the former case all the additional spending adds directly to the gross national product. The social value of the additional government expenditures may be relatively low, however. If the projects are poorly planned or projects are funded whose benefits are more political than economic, then the long-term benefit to society may be very limited.

## The Structural versus the Cyclical Budget Deficit

The federal government's annual fiscal position is determined by comparing government revenues with government expenditures. If the latter exceeds the former, there is a budget deficit, and in the opposite situation there is a budget surplus. For much of the post–World War II era, the federal government has operated with a budget deficit (See table 7–1).

One can separate the effects on the deficit of policy changes from the effects of the business cycle by calculating what the federal surplus or deficit would be given a standard or natural rate of unemployment. An unemployment rate of 6 percent is commonly used as an approximation of the natural rate of unemployment. This is lower than the rate reached at the trough of a recession but higher than the rate reached at the peak of the expansion during some recent economic fluctuations.

The budget surplus or deficit that the federal government incurs given the natural rate of unemployment is called the *structural deficit*. Changes in the structural deficit are interpreted as representing changes in policies regarding taxes, transfer payments, and government purchases. During recessions the actual deficit is greater than the structural deficit because of the decline in tax revenues and rise in government transfer payments.

**Table 7–1**
**Federal Receipts, Outlays, Surplus or Deficit, Selected Fiscal Years, 1940–1987**
*(billions of dollars)*

| Year | Receipts | As % of GNP | Expenditures | As % of GNP | Surplus or Deficit (−) | As % of GNP |
|------|----------|-------------|--------------|-------------|------------------------|-------------|
| 1940 | 6.5 | 6.8 | $ 9.5 | 9.9 | −2.9 | 3.0 |
| 1945 | 45.2 | 21.2 | 92.7 | 43.6 | −47.6 | 22.4 |
| 1950 | 39.4 | 14.8 | 42.6 | 16.0 | −3.1 | 1.2 |
| 1955 | 65.5 | 17.0 | 68.4 | 17.7 | −3.0 | 0.7 |
| 1960 | 92.5 | 18.3 | 92.2 | 18.2 | 0.3 | 0.0 |
| 1965 | 116.8 | 17.4 | 118.2 | 17.6 | −1.4 | 0.2 |
| 1970 | 192.8 | 19.5 | 195.6 | 19.8 | −2.8 | 0.2 |
| 1975 | 279.1 | 18.3 | 332.3 | 21.8 | −53.2 | 3.5 |
| 1979 | 463.3 | 18.9 | 503.5 | 20.6 | −40.2 | 1.6 |
| 1980 | 517.1 | 19.4 | 590.9 | 22.1 | −73.8 | 2.8 |
| 1981 | 599.3 | 20.1 | 678.2 | 22.7 | −78.9 | 2.6 |
| 1982 | 617.8 | 19.7 | 745.7 | 23.8 | −127.9 | 4.1 |
| 1983 | 600.6 | 18.1 | 808.3 | 24.3 | −207.8 | 6.3 |
| 1984 | 666.5 | 18.1 | 851.8 | 23.1 | −185.3 | 5.0 |
| 1985 | 734.1 | 18.6 | 946.3 | 24.0 | −212.3 | 5.4 |
| 1986 | 769.1 | 18.5 | 989.8 | 23.8 | −220.7 | 5.3 |
| 1987 | 842.4 | 19.1 | 1015.6 | 23.0 | −173.2 | 3.9 |

Source: U.S. Department of Commerce, *Economic Report of the President, 1987* (Washington, D.C.: U.S. Government Printing Office, 1987), p. 331.

The difference between the actual and structural deficits is called the *cyclical deficit*. When unemployment rises above 6 percent, the cyclical deficit becomes positive since the actual deficit exceeds the structural deficit. When unemployment falls below 6 percent, the actual deficit is less than the structural deficit. At such times the cyclical deficit is negative.

## The Growing Structural Deficit

It is generally agreed that the cyclical component of the federal deficit is less of a problem than the structural portion. What concerns many economists is the way the structural deficit has grown even as the cyclical deficit has fallen due to a steady upswing in business activity since late 1982. For example, the cyclical component of the deficit fell by $44 billion between 1982 and 1984.[7] Yet the actual federal deficit rose by $58 billion. A $102 billion increase in the structural deficit more than wiped out the budgetary benefits of the strong 1983–1984 economic recovery. Moreover, budget deficits of $175 to $200 billion occurred in 1985, 1986, and 1987, even with continued economic growth.

## Federal Expenditures and the Budget Deficit

Most economists cite the large-scale three-year phased reduction of personal and corporate taxes enacted in 1981 as the cause of the massive increase in structural deficits. Conservative economists, however, blame the deficit increase on excessive government spending. Initially, table 7–1 seems consistent with the conservative view since from 1982–1987 expenditures averaged 23–24 percent of GNP, an increase of nearly 3 percentage points from the 21.2 percent average of the 1970–1979 decade. In contrast, federal receipts in 1982–1987 averaged 18–19 percent of GNP, exactly the same as the 1970–1979 average. This explanation of the cause of recent budget deficits is incomplete, however, because without the Reagan tax changes, the share of federal receipts would have been 22.6 percent of GNP instead of 19.6 percent.[8] Thus, the tax reduction also played a large role in increasing the deficit.

The key changes in the distribution of federal spending between 1978 and 1986 are as follows:[9]

1. The share of defense spending rose substantially from 4.8 to 6.6 percent of GNP.
2. The share of Social Security benefits rose from 4.2 to 4.7 percent of GNP, reflecting the fact that Social Security benefits are indexed to the increase in the Consumer Price Index.

3. The share of Medicare expenditures rose from 1.0 to 1.7 percent of GNP, reflecting increased utilization of health benefits by elderly participants and the limited success in controlling health care costs.
4. The share of net interest payments rose from 1.5 to 3.2 percent of GNP, reflecting high interest rates and a growing cumulative debt.
5. The share of nondefense programs (except Social Security, Medicare, and net interest) declined by 1.8 percent of GNP.

## Effects of the Economy on the Federal Budget

Changes in real income, inflation, and interest rates affect both federal spending and receipts without any change in current fiscal policy. Estimates of these effects are summarized in table 7–2. Changes in economic conditions also affect the demand for federal spending. For example, an increase in real income reduces government outlays, increases receipts, and reduces the deficit by the sum of these two effects. An increase in real income, however, may also increase the demand for new or current federal services and transfers, so the net effect of higher real income can lead to higher federal expenditure.

Table 7–2
Sensitivity of the Budget to Changes in Economic Conditions, Fiscal Years 1986 and 1987[a]

| | Fiscal Year | |
|---|---|---|
| Item | 1986 | 1987 |
| *1 percentage point reduction in real GNP growth:* | | |
| Change in outlays | 0.2 | −1.1 |
| Change in receipts | −3.4 | −13.6 |
| Change in deficit | 3.6 | 14.7 |
| *1 percentage point reduction in inflation:* | | |
| Change in outlays | 0 | −1.5 |
| Change in receipts | −3.5 | −13.3 |
| Change in deficit | 3.5 | 11.8 |
| *1 percentage point higher unemployment rate:* | | |
| Change in outlays | 2.8 | 4.4 |
| Change in receipts | 0 | 0 |
| Change in deficit | 2.8 | 4.4 |
| *1 percentage point increase in interest rates:* | | |
| Change in outlays | 3.3 | 9.7 |
| Change in receipts | .5 | 1.1 |
| Change in deficit | 2.8 | 8.6 |

Source: Unpublished data from Office of Management and Budget and Council of Economic Advisers.

[a]Change assumed to begin in January 1986.

Table 7–2 indicates the estimated effects on outlays, receipts, and the deficit from changes in real GNP growth, inflation, the unemployment rate, and interest rates, assuming each change occurs beginning January 1986. The table shows the independent effect on the budget from a change in each variable; of course, a movement in one would normally occur concomitantly with changes in the others.

Clearly, variations in real growth and inflation can have large effects on government expenditures, receipts, and the deficit without any change in fiscal policy. Policy can, however, affect the responsiveness of the budget to economic conditions. For example, the indexation of individual income tax brackets that was incorporated in recent tax legislation reduces the sensitivity of receipts to changes in the inflation rate. A greater proportion of outlays are also now indexed. As a result, the size of the budget deficit is now much less sensitive to a change in the inflation rate than previously.

## Fiscal Policy, 1974–1980

In early 1974 the price of foreign oil was increased very substantially by the OPEC countries. This price increase, as well as considerable increases in farm prices, caused a rapid increase in inflation. During 1974 consumer prices rose about 12 percent. At the same time, the nation's real output fell, as the economy slid into the most serious recession since World War II. The result was a marked increase in unemployment. By March 1975 the unemployment rate was 8.7 percent, as compared with 4.9 percent in December 1973.

Faced with a combination of excessive unemployment and high inflation, President Ford signed in March 1975 a bill that resulted in a tax reduction of $23 billion. The economy began to revive in mid-1975, and unemployment fell from 8.7 percent in March 1975 to 7.5 percent in March 1976. Stagflation (the combination of a high unemployment rate and a high rate of inflation) continued, however.

In 1977 the federal government ran a budget deficit of about $50 billion; the full employment or structural deficit was about $30 billion. In January 1978 President Carter proposed personal tax reductions of $24 billion. However, during 1978 the rate of inflation increased sharply, and approached 10 percent per year. Since the inflation rate was higher than expected, the Carter administration reduced its proposed tax cut to $20 billion, and Congress ultimately passed a $19 billion tax cut.

In spite of increased inflation, fiscal policy did not attempt to significantly reduce aggregate demand. The deficit in 1978 was about $30 billion; the structural deficit was over $10 billion. There was a continuing debate within the administration over whether the inflation rate could be reduced substantially without causing a recession. In 1980, there was a six-month period of recession, but it was too brief to cause a substantial reduction in inflation. As in previous years, the federal government ran a substantial full-employment deficit.

## Fiscal Policy, 1981–1984

The cornerstone of the Reagan administration's tax policy, the Economic Recovery Tax Act (ERTA), was signed into law in August 1981. This act mandated major changes in both the individual and corporation income tax.

It provided for an across-the-board reduction in individual income tax rates amounting to 23 percent at the end of three years and an immediate reduction in the top bracket rate from 70 to 50 percent. The new law also established that, beginning in 1985, the tax brackets, exemption amounts, and the zero-bracket level would be indexed annually for inflation. This change ensured that inflation would not erode the ERTA tax reductions by pushing individuals into higher tax brackets (the so-called bracket creep phenomenon).

Reduced marginal tax rates were designed to increase incentives for supplying labor and acquiring training and education. There was a shift in emphasis away from using the tax system to redistribute income.

Responding to a widely held concern that the pace of capital formation had been insufficient, ERTA allowed accelerated depreciation of new capital assets and a system of expanded investment tax credits. Both of these provisions decreased the effective tax burden on new investment and thus provided an incentive for increased capital formation. To encourage saving, ERTA extended the individual retirement account program to individuals covered by employer-sponsored retirement plans and increased the maximum annual contribution from $1,500 to $2,000.

The Tax Equity and Fiscal Responsibility Act of 1982 (TEFRA) modified some of the effective tax reductions granted to businesses under ERTA. One of the objectives was to reduce the tax benefits of the investment tax credit and the accelerated cost recovery system so that they would not be more generous than an immediate write-off. Although this act repealed further accelerations of depreciation allowances scheduled for 1985 and 1986, the ERTA depreciation schedules for 1981–1984 were left basically intact.

## Fiscal Policy, 1985–1987

The current economic expansion marks the first occasion in the postwar period when federal deficits have exceeded 5 percent of GNP (see table 7–

1). It is also the first time that very large deficits have persisted into the third and fourth and fifth years of an expansion. At comparable periods during the cyclical upswings of the 1960s and 1970s, the federal deficit, as a share of GNP, was generally less than one-half the level of 1985–1987. The proportion of federal spending in GNP has continued on an upward trend, while for reasons discussed previously, the secular trend in the share of federal revenues has remained roughly constant.

Persistent large federal deficits throughout an economic expansion could pose a difficult dilemma for macroeconomic policy in the event of a significant economic downturn. As mentioned earlier, federal receipts automatically decline and transfer payments expand during a contraction. Either a highly restrictive fiscal policy would need to be adopted during a recession to prevent a further increase in the federal deficit, or the share of the deficit in GNP would need to be permitted to increase to levels not previously experienced during peacetime in the United States. At present there is no reason to expect a recurrence of the economic difficulties that contributed to the strong contractions of 1974–1975 and 1980–1982. It is very risky, however, to permit the persistence of large federal deficits throughout an economic expansion because of the dilemma such deficits could create if a recession did occur.

The Tax Reform Act of 1986 (TRA) makes further important changes in the economy's tax structure. First, it further reduces the marginal tax rates for most taxpayers below the levels achieved with the 1981 and 1982 tax legislation (see table 7–3.)

The largest absolute decline in tax rates occurs for those relatively high-

Table 7–3
**Marginal Personal Income Tax Rates for Four-Person Families, Selected Years, 1965–1988**
*(percent)*

| Year | One-Half Median Income | Median Income | Twice Median Income |
|------|------------------------|---------------|---------------------|
| 1965 | 14 | 17 | 22 |
| 1970 | 15 | 20 | 26 |
| 1975 | 17 | 22 | 32 |
| 1980 | 18 | 24 | 43 |
| 1986 | 14 | 22 | 38 |
| 1988 | 15 | 15 | 28 |

Source: Unpublished data, Office of Tax Analysis, U.S. Department of the Treasury.
Note: Excludes Social Security taxes and state and local income taxes.

income families who receive twice the median income. These families are earning approximately $60,000 a year.

The rate reductions are made possible in part because of an expanded definition of taxable personal income. The latter now includes the following sources of income: all long-term capital gains, state and local sales taxes, nonmortgage consumer interest payments, and miscellaneous itemized deductions that are less than 2 percent of adjusted gross income. This expanded concept of income is partially offset by substantial increases in the standard deduction and personal exemption. By 1988 the personal exemption is nearly doubled and the standard deduction is increased 36 percent for joint returns and 21 percent for single returns.[10]

An important feature of TRA is its strong limitation on tax-sheltered activities, which expanded greatly in the past decade. The elimination of the capital gains preference, the deceleration of tax depreciation deductions, more stringent limitations on investment interest deductions, and the lowering of marginal tax rates all serve indirectly to make tax shelters less attractive.

The tax shelter limitations not only make the personal income tax more equitable, but they should also result in more economically efficient investment decisions. Investments that previously provided opportunities for tax avoidance must now be evaluated in terms of their own intrinsic value. These funds should now have a tendency to flow into those sectors where expected net returns are greatest.

## Monetary and Fiscal Policy and the Trade Deficit

The deterioration of the U.S. trade balance has been a major problem during the current economic recovery. U.S. real net exports of goods and services declined sharply after 1981 to a deficit equivalent of more than 4 percent of real GNP in 1986. The growing U.S. trade deficit is often cited as a principal cause of the slowdown of real GNP growth since mid-1984.

The current account deficit—the excess of imports of goods and services over exports, plus net transfers to foreign residents—increased from $9 billion in 1982 to an estimated $145 billion in 1986. Almost all of this change is attributable to an increase in the merchandise trade deficit, which rose to nearly $150 billion in 1986 (see table 7–4).

The increase in the U.S. trade deficit is a macroeconomic phenomenon. Imports have grown strongly and exports have stagnated primarily because of the strong growth of the U.S. economy relative to other countries, the difficulties faced by many developing countries in managing their external debts, and the fall in U.S. price competitiveness associated with the large appreciation of the dollar between 1980 and 1985. Underlying these devel-

**Table 7–4**
**U.S. International Transactions, 1970–1986**
*(millions of dollars)*

| Year | Merchandise | | | Investment Income | | | Balance on Current Account |
|------|---------|---------|------|----------|----------|--------|----------------|
| | Exports | Imports | Net | Receipts | Payments | Net | |
| 1970 | 42,469 | 39,866 | 2,603 | 11,747 | 5,516 | 6,231 | 2,311 |
| 1975 | 107,088 | 98,185 | 8,903 | 25,531 | 12,564 | 12,787 | 18,116 |
| 1976 | 114,745 | 123,228 | −9,483 | 29,286 | 13,311 | 15,975 | 4,207 |
| 1977 | 120,816 | 151,907 | −31,091 | 32,179 | 14,217 | 17,692 | −14,511 |
| 1978 | 142,054 | 176,001 | −33,947 | 42,245 | 21,680 | 20,565 | −15,427 |
| 1979 | 184,473 | 212,009 | −27,536 | 64,132 | 32,960 | 31,172 | −991 |
| 1980 | 224,269 | 249,749 | −25,480 | 72,506 | 42,120 | 30,386 | 1,873 |
| 1981 | 237,085 | 265,063 | −27,978 | 86,411 | 52,329 | 34,082 | 6,339 |
| 1982 | 211,198 | 247,642 | −36,444 | 83,539 | 54,883 | 28,666 | −9,131 |
| 1983 | 201,820 | 268,900 | −67,080 | 77,251 | 52,410 | 24,841 | −46,604 |
| 1984 | 219,900 | 332,422 | −112,522 | 86,221 | 67,469 | 18,752 | −106,466 |
| 1985 | 214,424 | 338,863 | −124,439 | 89,991 | 64,803 | 25,188 | −117,677 |
| 1986[a] | 220,000 | 364,000 | −144,000 | 90,000 | 66,000 | 24,000 | −140,000 |

Source: U.S. Department of Commerce, *Economic Report of the President, 1987* (Washington, D.C.: U.S. Government Printing Office, 1987), p. 358.
[a]estimated.

opments are several macroeconomic imbalances, including the deterioration of the U.S. saving-investment balance that has resulted from the failure of the federal government to bring its expenditures in line with revenues.

For the United States the crowding out of net exports occurred when higher interest rates pushed up the value of the foreign exchange rate—that is, the value of the dollar—in terms of other currencies between 1980 and 1985. As the dollar became more valuable, foreigners had to pay more in terms of their own currencies in order to buy U.S. exports. Consumers and business firms had to pay fewer dollars to purchase imported goods.

The U.S. government budget deficit not only had profound effects on the American manufacturing and farm sectors, but also influenced economic activity in many foreign nations. Expansionary fiscal policy raised interest rates and the value of the dollar. While foreigners experienced higher sales as U.S. imports rose in response to the appreciated dollar, foreign economies were depressed by the effects of higher U.S. interest rates. This tended to raise foreign interest rates and in turn reduce investment and consumption spending abroad. As indicated above, in less developed countries with heavy debts to banks in the industrialized world, high interest rates raised the burden of repayment and brought several nations to near default.

The relative attractiveness of U.S. and foreign investments and securities depends on the *interest rate differential*, which is defined as the average U.S. interest rate minus the average foreign interest rate. When the U.S. interest rate increases relative to the foreign interest rate, foreigners find U.S. securities attractive, they demand additional dollars to purchase them, and the foreign exchange rate of the dollar is bid up by the foreign exchange traders.

The period of lowest real interest rates in the 1970s coincided with periods when the dollar was low. The era of high interest rates after 1980 was accompanied by an appreciation of the dollar. While changes in the interest rate cannot predict every fluctuation in the value of the dollar, it accounts for most of the variation.

For example, monetary policy became highly restrictive in 1979 and by 1981 interest rates reached the highest levels of the postwar period, contributing to the severity of the 1981–1982 recession. In spite of the recession, real interest rates remained high during 1981–1985 because of the need for funds to finance the growing budget deficit. This, as discussed earlier, contributed to the appreciation in the value of the dollar and the concomitant merchandise trade deficit.

Slower economic growth in 1985–1987 resulted in an easier monetary policy and a decline in the U.S. real interest rates. This was associated with a decline in the value of the dollar, which in late 1987 and early 1988 began to be reflected in a reduction in the trade deficit.

## The Savings-Investment Balance

The deterioration of the U.S. international payments position has also been associated with movements in national saving and investment. The U.S. deficit in goods and services trade indicates that total spending on goods and services exceeds U.S. production of goods and services. This necessarily implies that the United States is absorbing foreign saving to finance the difference between expenditures and income, or equivalently, that U.S. investment exceeds U.S. saving. For example, in 1986, gross national saving was $537 billion; gross private investment was $686 billion. The difference was financed by a net capital inflow of nearly $150 billion from abroad.

Between 1981 and 1986 the national saving rate fell more than 4 percentage points (see table 7–5). This drop has made the United States increasingly dependent on net capital inflows to finance U.S. investment. In 1986 net capital inflows—and the associated buildup of foreign claims on the United Sates—equaled one-half of U.S. net capital formation. To the extent that the drop in the national saving rate is unfavorable, this dependence on net capital inflows to finance U.S. investment is disconcerting. Part

Table 7–5
National Savings, Investment, and Net Capital Inflow
(*as percent of GNP*)

| Year | Gross Private Saving | Government Saving | Gross National Saving | Net Capital Inflow | Gross Private Domestic Investment |
|------|------|------|------|------|------|
| 1979 | 17.8 | 0.5 | 18.3 | −0.1 | 18.1 |
| 1980 | 17.5 | −1.3 | 16.3 | −0.3 | 16.0 |
| 1981 | 18.0 | −1.0 | 17.1 | −0.2 | 16.9 |
| 1982 | 17.6 | −3.5 | 14.1 | 0.0 | 14.1 |
| 1983 | 17.4 | −3.8 | 13.6 | 1.1 | 14.7 |
| 1984 | 17.9 | −2.7 | 15.2 | 2.4 | 17.6 |
| 1985 | 17.2 | −3.4 | 13.8 | 2.7 | 16.5 |
| 1986[a] | 16.2 | −3.4 | 12.8 | 3.5 | 16.3 |

Source: Unpublished data, Bureau of Economic Analysis, U.S. Department of Commerce.
[a]Estimated.

of the decline in the national saving rate has resulted from the failure to bring government expenditures in line with revenues. Thus, to a degree, the increased dependence on capital inflows to finance U.S. investment should be viewed as a by-product of a fiscal position that should be corrected by reducing the share of federal expenditures in GNP.

## The Gramm-Rudman-Hollings Act

The Gramm-Rudman-Hollings Act of 1985 provided for annual reductions in the budget deficit from $171.9 billion in fiscal year 1986 to zero in fiscal year 1991. The act established procedures to reduce deficits to the annual maximum levels by the mandatory sequestration of funds.[11]

The amount and percentage of required reduction was to be determined by the comptroller general based on a joint Office of Management and Budget (OMB) Congressional Budget Office (CBO) report. This report would estimate the fiscal year's budget deficit, discuss expected economic conditions, and present data on anticipated federal program expenditures.

The comptroller general was to issue a report indicating the amount of reduction to be made in each nondefense and defense program, project, or activity. The total reduction was to be equally divided between defense and nondefense programs. Except for programs with special regulations, equal percentage reductions were to be made. Thus, all defense programs were to be reduced by a constant percentage and nondefense programs cut back by their own uniform percentage.

Under the sequestration procedure, outlays were not reduced directly. Rather, redirections were made in budgetary resources and the associated outlay savings were estimated. For fiscal year 1986 the OMB/CBO joint report estimated that budgetary resources would have to be reduced by $33.2 billion (reductions of $24.3 billion in spending authority, $1.6 billion in direct loan obligations, and $7.3 billion in loan guarantees) in order to achieve the required $11.7 billion in outlay reductions.[12]

The 1985 Balanced Budget Act required that half the outlay reductions come from defense programs and the other half come from nondefense programs, as indicated above. The across-the-board reductions were determined by applying one uniform percentage (4.3) for domestic programs, and another (4.9) for defense programs. The cutback percentages differed principally because the size for the defense and nondefense budget bases subject to the uniform reductions differed by about $5 billion.

A number of types of expenditures (including interest on the public debt, Social Security, veterans' compensation and pensions, Medicaid, Aid to Families with Dependent Children, and food stamps) were not subject to sequestration. The sequestration process and related restrictions could also be suspended by Congress in case of recession.

On July 7, 1986 the Supreme Court struck down a major provision of the Gramm-Rudman-Hollings Act. In a seven-to-two decision, the Court held that the automatic mechanism for cutting spending, which is a basic element of the act, violated the Constitution's separation of powers by encroaching on the president's authority to execute the laws.[13]

The court invalidated the provision because it gave the comptroller general, who is subject to removal by Congress, the *executive* power to estimate, allocate, and order the spending cuts needed to meet deficit targets set by the law.

In September 1987 the president signed "Gramm-Rudman-Hollings II."[14] Under the new law the authority to issue the order sequestering funds is vested in the OMB director—an executive officer—rather than in the comptroller general. In addition, the revised legislation changes the deficit targets beginning with fiscal year (FY) 1988 and extends them for two years as follows:[15]

FY/1988: $144 billion
FY/1989:  136 billion
FY/1990:  100 billion
FY/1991:   64 billion
FY/1992:   28 billion
FY/1993:    0 billion

The revised law retains the basic formula under which half the required outlay reductions must come from defense programs and the other half from nondefense programs.

Gramm-Rudman-Hollings II also restores flexibility with respect to national defense programs. Thus, the president is permitted to exempt military personnel accounts fully or partially from the defense budget base that is subject to sequestration. The effect of this provision would be to increase the uniform percentage reduction made in all remaining defense accounts so that the total required defense outlay reduction would not change.

## Fiscal Policy and the Gramm-Rudman-Hollings Act

One of the biggest concerns relating to the Gramm-Rudman-Hollings Act is its effect on discretionary fiscal policy. Although the revised law indicates that its provisions may be suspended during recessions, it is not clear that the suspension procedures can be put into effect quickly enough to avoid having an important procyclical impact. Moreover, since economists have a relatively poor record in forecasting economic downturns, it is not likely that the deficit reduction procedures of the act could be suspended until a recession was well underway.

In addition, there is insufficient provision for suspending provisions of the act when economic growth is very slow and unemployment is rising. Such "growth recessions" occur from time to time (see chapter 2), and discretionary fiscal policy is one government tool for minimizing their effects.

One alterative to the Gramm-Rudman-Hollings Act is a policy that was first discussed during the Kennedy administration. That policy requires balancing the budget over the course of the business cycle. If such a policy were in effect, a budget deficit could occur during a period of slow or declining economic activity and a surplus could be realized during a period of expansion and prosperity. As long as the budget was balanced over the course of the business cycle, there would be no net increase in the budget deficit over time. This would seem to be a more flexible policy than is to be anticipated with the Gramm-Rudman-Hollings Act.

However, the Gramm-Rudman-Hollings Act is less extreme than the constitutional amendment that President Reagan requested in his January 1987 State of the Union Message. The constitutional amendment would prohibit the federal government from operating at a deficit—it would mandate a balanced budget. Such an amendment would have to be approved by two-thirds of the members of both houses of Congress and ratified by three-fourths of the state legislatures.

The major problem with a constitutional amendment prohibiting a budget deficit is that it would virtually eliminate the concept of discretionary fiscal policy. The government would be limited to two options: (1) balancing the budget (so that revenues were approximately equal to expenditures), and (2) operating with a budget surplus.

It is not likely that Congress would be willing to have its expenditure and revenue making powers limited by a constitutional amendment.

Moreover, the requirement that the budget be balanced even in a severe recession would mean that government expenditures would be forced to be curtailed at precisely the time that federal tax revenues are falling. Such a policy would only intensify the recession. In addition, it would put all of the countercyclical policy burden on the monetary sector. Monetary policy is generally considered to be more effective in combating the ravages of inflation than in stimulating an economy that is mired in recession.

## Summary

Fiscal policy refers to taxation and expenditure policies and concomitantly to budget surpluses and deficits. Automatic stabilizers are an important feature of the overall fiscal process. Requiring no discretionary action, tax receipts change automatically when income changes. The same stabilizing effect is created by transfer payments that automatically grow as income falls.

Because automatic stabilizers never *fully* offset the instabilities of an economy, an important role exists for discretionary fiscal policy. Public works and other expenditures on goods and services, however, can involve such time lags in becoming effective as to make them useless as a means of cushioning short recessions. Discretionary variations in transfer expenditures and tax rates have greater short-run flexibility, but may be offset by changes in personal saving.

It is widely agreed that the size of the cyclical component of the federal deficits is less of a long-term problem than the structural component. What concerns many economists is the way the structural deficit has grown even as the cyclical deficit has fallen. For example, the cyclical component of the deficit fell by $44 billion between 1982 and 1984. Yet the actual federal deficit rose by $58 billion. A $102 billion increase in the structural deficit more than wiped out the budgetary benefits of the strong 1983–1984 economic recovery. Moreover, the increasing structural deficit was partially responsible for the rise in interest rates, which attracted capital from abroad. The capital inflow helped cause appreciation in the exchange rate of the dollar vis-à-vis other currencies. This exchange rate appreciation was a major cause of the trade deficit: U.S. exports became too expensive to remain competitive on world markets.

The Gramm-Rudman-Hollings Act mandates reductions in the budget deficit. The revised act requires that budget deficits be eliminated by 1993. Many economists are concerned that the act greatly limits any discretionary fiscal policy in the event of a recession.

# Notes

1. M. O. Clements, "The Quantitative Impact of Automatic Stabilizers," *Review of Economics and Statistics* 42 (February 1960): 60.
2. Ibid.
3. S. J. Maisel, "Timing and Flexibility of a Public Works Program." *Review of Economics and Statistics* 31 (May 1949); Albert Ando and E. Carey Brown, "Lags in Fiscal Policy," in *Stabilization Policies* (Englewood Cliffs, N.J.: Prentice Hall, 1963).
4. Gary Fromm and Lawrence Klein, "A Comparison of Eleven Econometric Models of the United States," *American Economic Review* 63 (May 1973): 391.
5. Robert Barro, "Are Government Bonds Net Wealth?" *Journal of Political Economy* 82 (November/December 1984): 1095–117.
6. Arthur Okin concluded in a 1971 study that the 1968 tax increase did limit consumer spending somewhat, but not enough to make a major impact on inflation. See Arthur Okun, *The Personal Tax Surcharge and Consumer Demand, 1968–1970*, vol. 3 of Brookings papers on Economic Activity (Washington, D.C.: The Brookings Institution, 1971).
7. U.S. Department of Commerce, *Economic Report of the President, 1986* (Washington, D.C.: U.S. Government Printing Office, 1986), p. 320.
8. Henry Wallich and Darrel Cohen, "Perspectives on U.S. Fiscal Policy," in *Festschrift in Honor of Professor Werner Ehrlicher* (Berlin: Duncker and Hermblot forthcoming), table 2.
9. U.S. Department of Commerce, *Economic Report of the President, 1987* (Washington, D.C.: U.S. Government Printing Office, 1987), p. 69.
10. Ibid., p. 83.
11. Allen Schick, "Explanation of the Balanced Budget and Emergency Deficit Control Act of 1985" (The Gramm-Rudman-Hollings Act), Congressional Research Service, Library of Congress, February 1986, p. 1.
12. Robert Keith, "Sequestration of Budgetary Resources for Fiscal Year 1986 under the 1985 Balanced Budget Act," Congressional Research Service, Library of Congress, September 1986, pp. 7–9.
13. Ibid., p. 22.
14. U.S. House of Representatives, *Increasing the Statutory Limit on the Public Debt*, 100th Cong., 1st sess., Rep. 100–313 (Washington D.C.; U.S. Government Printing Office, 1987), pp. 1–37.
15. Ibid., p. 44.

# Index

Abramowitz, Moses, 24
Acceleration principle: basic description of, 40–43; business cycles and, 40–43, 45–49, 54; interaction of multiplier with, 45–48, 54
Aid to Families with Dependent Children, 122
Automobile strike of 1970, 64

Balance-of-payments (trade) deficits, 9, 63, 64–65, 118–120, 124
Banking Act of 1980, 98
Banking Act of 1982, 98
Barro-Ricardo equivalence-theorem, 111
Borrowed reserves, 92
Brenner, M. Harvey, 83, 84, 86, 88
Budget deficits, 1, 9, 75, 102–103, 115–117, 119; federal expenditures and, 113–114; Gramm-Rudman-Hollings Act of 1985, 121–123, 125; growth of, 113; Reagan's proposed balanced-budget constitutional amendment, 123–124; structural versus cyclical, 111–113, 124
Burns, Arthur, 11, 12, 13
*Business Conditions Digest* (U.S. Department of Commerce), 6
*Business Cycle Developments* (U.S. Department of Commerce), 6
Business cycles: acceleration principle and, 40–43, 45–49, 54; actual duration of, 16–17, 25–26; basic description of, 11–12; Cassel theory of, 38; disinflation and, 18, 32; effects of, 9, 77–88; growth cycles compared to, 23; Hawtrey theory of, 31–32; Hayek theory of, 33–35; health status and, 9, 77, 83–87, 88; Hicks theory of, 47–50; inflation and, 18, 30, 31, 33, 34, 53; interest rates and, 19, 31–32, 35, 36, 38, 39, 40, 51, 53;

international aspects of, 22, 26; inventories and, 23–25, 26, 31; Juglar theory of, 14–15; Keynes theory of, 9, 29, 38–40, 54; Kitchen theory of, 14, 15; Kondratieff theory of, 14, 15, 16; models of financial instability and, 51–53; money supply and, 31–35, 50–51; multiplier and, 43–48, 54; principal features of, 18–19, 21, 26; recent developments in, 22–23; Schumpeter theory of, 12–13, 14–15, 29–30, 40–41; Spiethoff theory of, 37–38; Tugan-Baranowsky theory of, 36–37; unemployment and, 9, 11, 13, 18, 19, 26, 31, 32, 35, 36, 37, 43, 49, 54, 77–88. *See also specific periods, e.g.,* Expansion of 1971-1973; Recession of 1981-1982

Carter, Jimmy, 93, 115–116
Cassel, Gustav, cycle theory of, 38
Central bank. *See* Federal Reserve System
Congressional Budget Office (CBO), 121–122
Consolidated Edison, 67
*Contribution to the Theory of the Trade Cycle, A* (Hicks), 47
Council of Economic Advisors, 6

Deficits: budget, 1, 9, 75, 102–103, 111–117, 119, 121–125; interest rates and, 119–120; trade (balance-of-payments), 9, 63, 64–65, 118–120, 124
Deflation. *See* Disinflation
Deregulation, 98–99, 107
Devaluation of the dollar, 7, 65, 106
Discount rate, 31, 63, 105
Disinflation: business cycles and, 18, 32; Federal Reserve System and, 99–103; optimal policy for, 101–103; recession

# About the Author

Alan L. Sorkin is professor and chairman of the Department of Economics at the University of Maryland, Baltimore County. He also holds appointments in the Department of Epidemiology and Social Medicine at the University of Maryland Medical School and the Department of International Health of The Johns Hopkins University, School of Hygiene and Public Health. He received his Ph.D. in economics from Johns Hopkins in 1966. Dr. Sorkin is the author of *American Indians and Federal Aid* (The Brookings Institution, 1971), and the following volumes published by Lexington Books: *Education, Unemployment and Economic Growth* (1974); *Health Economics: An Introduction* (1975; revised second edition, 1984); *Health Economics in Developing Countries* (1976); *Health Manpower: An Economic Perspective* (1977); *The Urban American Indian* (1978); *The Economics of the Postal System* (1980); *Economic Aspects of Natural Hazards* (1982); and *Health Care and the Changing Economic Environment* (1986). He has also written a number of articles focusing on the economics of human resources.